faith with Wings

Also by AmyLu Riley

Faith with Grit for the Not-Yet Healed
Stay: Why I'm Still Here, A Spiritual Memoir
Jesus as Healer: Miracles and Meditations in Luke

Join the email list
https://amylu-riley.com/subscribe

AmyLu Riley

Published by
AmyLu Riley
Evansville, Indiana
United States of America
https://amylu-riley.com

Faith with Wings
Copyright © 2020 by AmyLu Riley

Published by AmyLu Riley
Evansville, Indiana, United States of America
books@amylu-riley.com

ISBN: 978-0-9973496-4-1 (paperback)
ISBN: 978-0-9973496-7-2 (ebook)
Library of Congress Control Number: 2019905882

First Edition, 2020

All rights reserved. No part of this publication may be reproduced, stored in a retrieval system, or transmitted in any form by any means—electronic, mechanical, photocopy, recording, or any other—except for brief quotations in printed reviews, without the prior written permission of the publisher.

Unless otherwise indicated, all Scripture quotations are taken from the Holy Bible, New Living Translation, copyright © 1996, 2004, 2015 by Tyndale House Foundation. Used by permission of Tyndale House Publishers, a division of Tyndale House Ministries, Carol Stream, Illinois 60188. All rights reserved.

Scripture quotations marked NKJV are taken from the New King James Version®. Copyright © 1982 by Thomas Nelson. Used by permission. All rights reserved.

Scripture quotations marked MSG are taken from THE MESSAGE, copyright © 1993, 2002, 2018 by Eugene H. Peterson. Used by permission of NavPress. All rights reserved. Represented by Tyndale House Publishers, a Division of Tyndale House Ministries.

Cover design: Richard Riley
Cover photo: Chris Sabor on Unsplash
Typefaces: Sorts Mill Gaudy by Barry Schwartz, Scriptina, Libre Franklin

Printed by Kindle Direct Publishing
Charleston, South Carolina, United States of America

For God, who loves me and is freeing me to soar

What is important is faith expressing itself in love.

Galatians 5:6

Contents

1. For the Love of God   13

2. Can God Be Trusted?   19

3. Demolition   37

4. Commissioned   41

5. Awakening   43

6. What Does God Want?   49

7. Case Not Closed   67

8. Seeing the Battlefield   75

9. Active Duty   85

10. Power   91

11. Loving Christ   95

12. My Isaac   101

    Note from the Author   109

    Acknowledgements   111

    Questions for Believers   113

    Notes   117

faith
with
Wings

1

For the Love of God

As the years continued to pass without complete healing, I sometimes felt a little resentful toward Paul.

First, because he got such *clear* revelation about the *reason* for his *thorn in the flesh*, whatever it was.[1] And second, because he apparently received an answer from God each time he prayed about it—even though it wasn't the response he had asked for.

> *... I have received such wonderful revelations from God. So to keep me from becoming proud, I was given a thorn in my flesh, a messenger from Satan to torment me and keep me from becoming proud.*
>
> *Three different times I begged the Lord to take it away. Each time he said, "My grace is all you need. My power works best in weakness."*
>
> 2 CORINTHIANS 12:7–9

Since God deals with each of us uniquely (John 21:22; Matthew 20:12), I knew it wasn't a good idea for me to zero in on this single instance of God's dealings with Paul and demand the same style of communication from God for myself. There were people who had prayed for far longer than I, who had *also* heard no such reply. But sometimes I just wished God would clue me in about what was going on in my life.

And then, one day, as I read Jesus's message to the church at Ephesus (Revelation 2:1–7), I realized that I had another problem—even bigger than being unhealed.

"You have patiently suffered for me without quitting.
But I have this complaint against you. You don't love me or each other as you did at first!"
REVELATION 2:3–4

I knew that Jesus could say the same thing about *my* love for him, and that he'd be right.

And I knew that had to change.

Cool Love

I do *love* God, of course, but—I have awakened to the realization—definitely not in the way I should. My love for God seems to be only in my *mind*, which is not the same as the love he *wants* me to have—love that pervades the heart, mind, and soul; love that spills out in action toward others. He wants the love described in 1 John 4:7–12.

I think Jesus's word *complaint* (in Revelation 2:4) pinpoints the cause. Without even being aware of it until now, I think *I* have harbored an unformed complaint against God. I haven't given it words, or a voice. I have kept my head down, and I have kept on. But I can see it in my heart: I am disappointed at the way I perceive God has chosen to deal with me. My *reality* has not yet fallen into line with my *expectations* of him, which I *thought* were based on Scripture.

Yet, it's not only that. The way God has handled his end of things has been painful, and pain itself has been a wedge.

I see from Scripture that I am not alone in that.

Job had complaints, too—a number of them. Although Job was *commended for his perseverance* (James 5:11)—just as the church of Ephesus was in Revelation 2—Job had *many* complaints against God, and he even *called* them that. (See Job 6:5; 7:11; 9:27; 10:1; 21:4; 23:2; and perhaps also 13:3, 15.) Job talked about being sick at heart and terrified (Job 23:16). He said that God had "wronged" him (Job 19:6) and "persecuted" him (Job 19:22); that God didn't answer him—or even look at him—when he cried to God (Job 30:20); and that God had become cruel toward him (Job 30:21). *And God confirmed that Job was right about all of that* (Job 42:7).

Jesus felt it, too. And even though Jesus *knew* the plan for his own suffering, *agreed* to it, and then willingly *submitted* to carrying it out, he also still *felt pain* at the way God dealt with him.

> *At about three o'clock, Jesus called out with a loud voice,* "Eli, Eli, lema sabachthani?" *which means* "My God, my God, why have you abandoned me?"
>
> MATTHEW 27:46

Jesus's pain had even been prophesied—and felt, in some measure—by David:

Why are you so far away when I groan for help?
Every day I call to you, my God, but you do not answer.
Every night I lift my voice, but I find no relief.
PSALM 22:1–2

But, of course, God didn't leave Jesus stuck in that pain. After Jesus's resurrection from the dead and appearances to the disciples, Jesus was later "taken up into heaven and sat down in the place of honor at God's right hand" (Mark 16:19)—a reality that is *quite the opposite* of abandonment by God.

If I can adjust my *expectations* to align correctly with *who God really is* and *what he actually does*—and if I can realize that I, too, will come *through* my own pain at *some* point—can I get through it all *loving him?*

Paul did. His suffering never seemed to interrupt his deep intimacy with God.

And, so, Jesus's words to the church in Ephesus convict me: *So, you think that what you've been through constitutes grounds for complaint against me? Listen to my complaint against you. Your love has cooled off.*

Maybe this is why Jesus said the greatest *commandment* is to love God (Matthew 22:37–38). Things that are easy and just come naturally usually don't need to be made into commandments. So if loving God is *the greatest commandment,* maybe it is also *the most difficult thing to do.*

The reasons I assumed I'd *ended up* in this state of cooled love seemed outside my control. Yet, it must still be *possible* to love God with all my heart, mind, and soul, or else Jesus wouldn't have spoken about it the way he did (Matthew 22:37; Revelation 2:3–4).

And even though obedience is not optional, but *imperative,* doesn't the mandate to love God point beyond mere rule-keeping to the reality that *love* is the preferred state in which to *live* in relationship with a God who *is* love?

I recognized that I *needed* to love God fully, *and I wanted to.* But how?

God, show me what to do to love you more!

I imagined all the wedges to my closeness with God—all of my *complaints*—being turned upside down, becoming fulcrums to leverage my suffering into the very thing that presses me closer to God's heart than I have ever been. Rather than be on the *defensive* against God in areas of my life that were painful to me, I would partner *with* him to go on the *offensive* against the gates of Hell.

It sounded good, but what could actually bring that vision to life? I asked God to help me.

I could not have foreseen the forms that help would take!

2

Can God Be Trusted?

It took me years to understand that my question *God, are you going to heal me?* was something of a red herring. It was valid, but the deeper question I needed the answer to was *Will I trust God even if he doesn't heal me?*

How simple, how very easy, it would be to trust a deity who gave me everything I could want for myself, including the healing that topped my list.

That kind of god wouldn't require any *real* trust at all. If I didn't have to wait, I knew everything that was going to happen, and everything was good and pleasant all the time, then there would be no opportunity—or even any need—for faith. In that scenario, I wouldn't even need *healing*, because nothing would have ever been allowed to happen to produce physical brokenness in the first place.

But how do I trust the actual God, the one who is *able* to do *everything*, but who hasn't—and who has long been known to operate that way?

"If we are thrown into the blazing furnace, the God whom we serve is able to save us. He will rescue us from your power, Your Majesty. But even if he doesn't, we want to make it clear to you, Your Majesty, that we will never serve your gods or worship the gold statue you have set up."
DANIEL 3:17–18

My focus keeps getting dragged down to the eye level of the problems and predicaments that are always ready to stare me down. And not only that, but I keep getting caught up in fixing my eyes on outcomes—the short-term kind that would wrap everything up neatly with a bow.

I also have another option, however. I *could* lift my eyes to the Lord who made the universe (Psalm 121:1–2); I *could* fix my eyes on the author and finisher of my faith (Hebrews 12:2).

Trust will have to be something that I *choose* to do. Although faith is *enabled* by God (Romans 12:3; 2 Peter 1:1; Philippians 1:29), I have to *will* to engage it, and then deliberately *choose* it—again and again, as many times as it takes.

But why would I choose to *trust* God unless I believe he is *trustworthy*?

The Evidence of Hope

I don't doubt that God *will* eventually keep Scriptural *promises* to me, but Scripture is pretty clear that there could be a long wait (see Hebrews 11:13).[1]

I can also believe that each of God's *answers* to me—or even his silence—is for a good reason.

And, yet, *promises* and *answers* are not the sum total of God to his people. Isn't the security of a relationship with God based on more than that? Doesn't it go deeper?

Isn't my trust in God based on the *person of God himself* in the past and in the present—on his character? On *knowing* that he is *always* good and loving—even *before* he delivers on promises, and *before* he answers? Doesn't fully trusting him require believing that in *everything* he permits while I am *waiting* for his answers and fulfilled promises, his *every* intention toward me is *always* good and loving?

It is *that* faith that gets strained almost to the breaking point at times. When things look and feel terrible, and I have no promise of relief in *this* life, and God seems silent—that's when my faith in him is in the fire.

Can he be trusted? Will I still believe in the goodness and love of a God who allows things to be done this way, when he has the power to intervene?

It's in—and because of—times like *this* that having faith in God's *character* as being *good* and *loving* will be the *real* evidence of my hope (Hebrews 11:1). Because those are the times when a seed planted by the Enemy can become a root of *distrust* of God's *character*.

The Enemy sows—and tends—the lie that *God can't be completely trusted; that my unhealed life doesn't demonstrate God's love, goodness, or care for me.*

It's an old, old lie.

Don't You Care?

The disciples woke him up, shouting, "Teacher, don't you care that we're going to drown?"
MARK 4:38

Of the three Gospels that record Jesus stilling a dangerous storm with his words, Mark includes a detail the other two do not.

Luke documents the announcement of trouble in the boat (Luke 8:24). Matthew adds the disciples' cries to be saved (Matthew 8:25). But Mark's account is the only one that records the shouted words *Don't you care?*

The disciples' loud question puts a finger on the grief that is *worse* than whatever suffering befalls me: the sinking feeling that, although God may be *working* in and through my circumstances—working out his will, building his kingdom, and adding to his glory—he might not *care* about what *his* agenda is doing *to me*.

Doesn't he care that I'm going to drown?

If I know God *does* care, and I'm convinced that I can trust in his attentive compassion, then I will be able to sleep when the storm comes against my boat and threatens to sink it. But if I'm not *sure* whether he cares—and it looks like he's not doing anything—I'll have my wary eyes on the waves, and my sad heart will be battered right along with the boat.

Getting That in Writing

Scripture says that it is precisely *because* God *loves* people that he was *willing* to go to such lengths—being born as a human; suffering betrayal, rejection, torture, and death—to *save* as many people as possible from otherwise certain eternal destruction (John 3:16–17). Jesus's sacrificial death is the ultimate manifestation and proof of God's care. God was willing to suffer *that* much to rescue humans. He has conclusively demonstrated—by his own sacrifice (1 John 4:8–10)—that he is *not* some aloof deity.

Yet, although I am convinced that he loves me in such a way as to give me the way to a better *eternity*, I still can't understand when that deep and sacrificial love doesn't appear to extend to the painful parts of *this* life that would be so easy for him to fix. Does God care *only* about eternity? After all, it's not as if God doesn't *understand* the human condition and what it's like to live *inside* of time, *with* suffering. He knows our suffering intimately *because he has carried it* (Isaiah 53:3–5).

It can be confusing, because God has *put into words* how *much* he cares about even the smallest details of his creation. In his response to Job (recorded in Job 38–39), God eloquently described his intricate care of an entire planet and its wild creatures—attention at a level of detail I cannot fathom. That account begs the question for me, as I wonder if it may have for Job: *If you care so much about all of your creation, then why don't you rush relief to me? Why are you willing to not seem to care about* my circumstances?

I'm not alone in asking. When Paul penned Romans 8:35–39, he was addressing believers whose suffering put them at risk of feeling separated from God's love. Paul had to *tell* believers that it wasn't *possible* for them to be separated from God's love. He had to spell it out for them in writing, because the powers of Hell were making a strong effort to ensure that the way believers' lives *looked* and *felt* told them a *different* story.

And there it is: There can be a difference between what I see and feel—how things *seem*, and what is actually *true*. After all, Scripture says that Jesus *loved* Martha and Mary and Lazarus, *even though* he stayed where he was instead of going to them to heal Lazarus. It really *looked like* Jesus was holding out on them.

> *The two sisters sent a message to Jesus telling him, "Lord, your dear friend is very sick."*
> *... although Jesus loved Martha, Mary, and Lazarus, he stayed where he was for the next two days.*
> JOHN 11:3, 5–6

But to judge truth through the lens of how life looks and feels from the *human* perspective is to look through the wrong end of the telescope. The story of Lazarus demonstrates that that's not the way to see *how things really are in the big picture.*

There was a vitally important *reason* that Jesus waited to go to them, and it was *not* that he did not care about Lazarus (John 11:33–38). Jesus was focused on accomplishing a work of God that was not possible for his loved ones to understand in the moment, of which Lazarus's resurrection from the dead would be a pivotal part.[2]

Yet, Jesus *loved* Lazarus and his family, and even as his work unfolded, he was *troubled* and even *angry* at the deep pain that sin had caused in his creation—the pain of all of the grief immediately before him, as well as the pain of the entire world. He, God in the flesh, cared so deeply that he *wept* outside the tomb *of the person he knew he was about to raise from the dead* (John 11:33, 35).

God's will is not uncaring or detached from our welfare. His will *encompasses* his care for humanity—*including me.*

But if God cares so deeply about the details of our lives and is so deeply moved at our individual suffering, why did he—*and why does he yet*—not do *all of it* another way?

Good God

During the years that my family kept rabbits, I learned that some mother rabbits inadvertently sit on their tiny offspring, crushing them in the course of taking care of them. It was always a shocking scene to discover.

And, so, when I came to Isaiah 53:10, I ran up against it hard.

> *But it was the LORD's good plan to crush him*
>   *and cause him grief.*
> *Yet when his life is made an offering for sin,*
>   *he will have many descendants.*
> *He will enjoy a long life,*
>   *and the LORD's good plan will prosper in his hands.*
>
> ISAIAH 53:10

Isaiah records that it was *God's* "good plan" to *crush* Jesus. Yet Jesus himself, *knowing that he would be crushed in this scenario*, said God is "truly good" (Mark 10:18). How does *that* compute?

Does the word *good* not mean what I think it means? *How* is this *good?*

The Rescue of Jesus

> *While Jesus was here on earth, he offered prayers and pleadings, with a loud cry and tears, to the one who could rescue him from death. And God heard his prayers because of his deep reverence for God.*
>
> HEBREWS 5:7

Since Jesus was crucified and died after praying these prayers, I used to consider them *unanswered* prayers. After all, didn't the fact that Jesus had died *mean* that the prayer had not been answered?

But then I noticed something: I had been measuring God's action against the standard of *prevention of suffering*. But the word used here in Scripture is one with the sense of *delivery* or *rescue*—of pulling someone *out* of a dire situation once they are already *in* it. And I see that that is exactly what God did—he pulled Jesus *out* of death (Acts 2:24)—something no other power could have done.

Jesus's prayer *had been* fully heard by God, *and* answered according to God's will. And based on Jesus's words to Peter, that's how Jesus interpreted the situation, too (John 18:11). *The Father was giving Jesus this cup to drink.*

God hadn't fallen back on some *second-best* answer to prayer rather than *the very best* answer to prayer. Nor had he silently disregarded Jesus's prayer.

The part of Jesus's prayers in Gethsemane that asked God to *take away* the coming suffering, if possible, *was* outweighed by his prayer that the Father's will be done instead of the Son's. God had *heard* Jesus's prayers requesting to avoid the coming suffering if there was a way to do that *and* accomplish God's will (John 11:42), but the crushing of Jesus had already been assigned as the will of God (Isaiah 53:10).

It was by going through this experience—not by going around it—that Jesus would be changed to become what God had *ordained* for him to be. And God wanted Jesus to become the Messiah. Far from doing *nothing* while Christ suffered, God was hearing Jesus, qualifying him, making him, and designating him to be the sole rescuer of the human race (Hebrews 5:8–10).

I suspect that enlarging my perspective to encompass eternal things is also the only way to internalize the truth that a God who *planned* to crush Christ (Isaiah 53:10; 1 Peter 1:11) *is truly good.*

I am going to need help with this.

Rescue 101

I have long wondered why God actually created humanity *despite* knowing what a painful mess it would be here.

I questioned why he created a race of people, despite *knowing* that humankind would (almost immediately) rebel against him and, as a result, subsequently suffer in a broken world in which *every* life would be in *need* of many kinds of healing, but would not always receive it (Ecclesiastes 3:1, 3).

But it appeared that that's what he did. And so, at the fall of humankind—and for a long time afterward—humanity was overrun by sin (Genesis 2:15–17; Genesis 3; Romans 7:21–24). Satan may have thought he had won. But then God mounted a rescue.

The law of Moses was unable to save us because of the weakness of our sinful nature. So God did what the law could not do. He sent his own Son in a body like we sinners have. And in that body God declared an end to sin's control over us by giving his Son as a sacrifice for our sins.
ROMANS 8:3

Who would have *ever* thought of the plan God devised to rescue the race of humankind (Romans 5:6–11)? And if someone ever *did* conceive of it before it was revealed by God, wouldn't they have quickly dismissed the idea as preposterous and impossible? Who would have ever imagined a god actually *doing* it—especially an all-powerful, royal father sending a beloved only son to do it? And who would have thought of any royal son willingly *going* to do it?

My first problem getting my head around *all* of this is that I have trouble comprehending that God decided to go ahead and create *this* world and bring the spirits of human beings into it, *fully knowing in advance* the horrible cost to *him* of saving even the *portion* of the race of humanity he would rescue (1 Peter 1:18–20).

God's own grief (Isaiah 53:10) in providing a rescue for even *some* of us wasn't even the whole cost of it, though. Jesus's words made it clear that the pain of *waiting* to end this age (until everyone possible is rescued; see 2 Peter 3:9) is a hard thing for him to endure:

"I have come to set the world on fire, and I wish it were already burning!"
LUKE 12:49

God loves us. He sees and *knows firsthand* how much this life hurts us (see John 11:33–35, 38), and he wants to get us safely home.

I can see that he *has* chosen to do it *this way*, but I am apparently totally missing the part of the story that would help me understand *why*. The answer *because he loved the world that much* (John 3:16) seems to me to just beg the question. I am like the two-year-old, with the incessant, looping reply to every answer given: "But why?"

I get stuck right there, a metaphorical sister of Lazarus. I become both Martha and Mary, pointing out to God in my suffering that *all of this pain could have been avoided if he had just ✓ done things differently* (John 11:21, 32). And Jesus stands there with me—himself angry, deeply troubled, and weeping (see John 11:33–35, 38, especially the NLT translation).

God, why make a race you knew would rebel, requiring rescue at the cost of your own Son's life? As Job and Solomon both said (Job 3; Ecclesiastes 4:3), wouldn't it have been better if humanity had never been born? With the cost to you so high to save just some people, why not forego even creating the human race?

I remained stuck, right there, for a long time: A little bit miffed at God for setting the whole thing up the way he apparently had. A little bit hurt that he hadn't showed up a lot sooner in my pain, especially when I'd repeatedly asked him to. A little standoffish about trusting the character of an omniscient and all-powerful being who thought that *all of this*—doing things *this* awful way—was really a good idea, a "good plan" (Isaiah 53:10).

And then I found something.

Discovering Plan A

In a verse I must have read dozens of times, I now noticed something for the first time: The costly *rescue* of this race of humans *wasn't* God's plan B, as I had long thought. *It was always plan A. He didn't just want us. He wanted to have to rescue us.*

> For God saved us and called us to live a holy life. He did this, not because we deserved it, but because that was his plan from before the beginning of time—to show us his grace through Christ Jesus.
> 2 TIMOTHY 1:9

God had made humans, not *despite* the cost to him, but *because* of it. *He wanted to save us, and so he put us into a situation where we would require saving.*[3]

This is *really* not the story I thought it was.

God created people *so that* he could be merciful to us (Romans 11:32). *All* of that was his plan from *before* the beginning of time—*before* humans sinned; before humans were *created*; before God spoke the world into existence.

I have been sure before that I could never understand the mind of God—and Scripture confirms that no human can (1 Corinthians 2:11; Romans 11:33). But now I am convinced once more: *I can never understand this God.* He wants to *have to come to my aid* in order to give me his grace—his kindness, gifts, and blessing. So he created a world and a race of beings in which he could carry out that kind of rescue.

So the *truth* is that God's creation of humankind was an idea planned from the beginning—*pitfalls included*, in order to create an opportunity for God to give something wonderful to those he chose in advance (Romans 8:30).

And there was still more.

A Secret, Revealed

The story doesn't even end with God giving to his human children, through Christ, something good that he wanted to give. The New Testament teaches that God's purpose in doing *that* was *always* to display his wisdom to entities in *another realm* (2 Timothy 1:9; Ephesians 3:10–11).

> *I was chosen to explain to everyone this mysterious plan that God, the Creator of all things, had kept secret from the beginning.*
>
> *God's purpose in all this was to use the church to display his wisdom in its rich variety to all the unseen rulers and authorities in the heavenly places. This was his eternal plan, which he carried out through Christ Jesus our Lord.*
>
> EPHESIANS 3:9–11

As that truth got into my mind and heart, and expanded there, I felt myself turning toward God in some new way. I still didn't understand *why* God would have *this* as his "eternal plan," but the truth—which has proven to be a far bigger and more squirming, live thing than I had ever suspected—opened my heart further to God's.

I considered this solid biblical truth: There is another whole *story* outside the layer of our earthbound story. God's purpose *is to demonstrate his wisdom to the unseen rulers and authorities in heavenly realms.* Our entire human existence is part of a plan to display God's wisdom—through Jesus, using the church—to an extraterrestrial audience.

How many layers *are* there to this story? And which layer explains *why* God finds it *necessary* to display his wisdom to those entities in heavenly realms? Which layer explains why God couldn't just *have* us and give us all the gifts he wanted to, without a scenario in which he must *rescue* us and all parties must suffer? Which layer explains why God *chose* a plan in which he gets to keep only some of his creation, and forfeits others (Isaiah 43:4; John 17:2, 6, 9, 12, 20, 24; 2 Thessalonians 1:9)?

Some layer of the story involving a heavenly court was the apparent seedbed of Job's earthly trouble. Yet, although Job was reassured by God on many points,[4] God apparently did *not* inform him of the goings-on of the heavenly court as they were occurring; we readers of the book of Job only know about it from the mentions in Job 1:6 and 2:1.

I suspect that if there were a *full* explanation that humans *could* understand of what precisely is going on with these "unseen rulers and authorities in the heavenly places," it might have been written by Paul, who was permitted to reveal, for the first time, that part of the mystery that he wrote about in Ephesians 3. While Paul's visions and revelations contained far more than he was permitted to share (2 Corinthians 12:1, 4), he is the one from whose letters we read of the "unseen rulers and authorities in the heavenly places" in Ephesians 3 and Ephesians 6; and of the "huge cloud of witnesses" in Hebrews 12:1.

Apparently, we are on a need-to-know basis, and we don't need to know more than the barest references to that realm, (such as those revealed in Luke 10:18, Daniel 10, and Revelation 12). Job may have best expressed reality when he observed that he had ventured into things too wonderful for him (Job 42:3). After all, look at the profound effect it had on Paul to see and hear those things from other realms that *he* was permitted to witness (2 Corinthians 12:1–7).

Yet, oddly enough, I now knew that I *didn't* need to know. That part of Job's own experience (Job 42:3–6) in which he laid down his line of questioning of God had always seemed a little too convenient for my taste, and somewhat annoying. But now, here I was, anyway. Once my understanding was opened to the magnitude of the many layers of reality at work above mine, my heart was opened to trust God from where I was, however deep inside them. Once I could see that *I could never see the last why*, I was oddly *reassured* by how very small, yet how ridiculously loved, God's people actually *are* in this story.

It had taken *so long* for me to finally see it this way. But the more I meditated on it, the more I became able to keep my grasp on my place in it: From his eternal existence outside of my space and time, God *is* operating out of *love* for me (1 John 4:10). He *does* have my good in mind. His character *can* be trusted.

If God says he is doing all of *this* to demonstrate his *wisdom* to some audience, then I can be assured of what will characterize this story, because God has already *described* his wisdom:

> *But the wisdom from above is first of all pure. It is also peace loving, gentle at all times, and willing to yield to others. It is full of mercy and the fruit of good deeds. It shows no favoritism and is always sincere.*
> JAMES 3:17

And so I make a choice. I decide to trust God's character, even before my eyes can see *how* he will bring good from *all* things (Romans 8:23–25, 28).[5]

The *lie* had said that *God can't be completely trusted, because my unhealed life doesn't demonstrate his love, goodness, or care for me.* But God had worked in *power* through his Word to break that lie with the *truth*.

It felt as if I had a better foundation now, something solid that he could build on.

I didn't know that there was anything else that needed tearing down.

3

Demolition

Her voice was raised. She sounded angry, but also far more: hurt, betrayed. She spoke directly to him, forcefully pronouncing in a loud and accusing tone that *she knew he was never going to heal her, because he* hadn't *healed her.*

I listened in horror, alarms shrilling in every system of my body. *What are you doing?! You can't speak to God that way! It just isn't done—not by someone who loves him!* I needed to intervene. I had to make her stop.

But there was nothing I could do. She had said it. It was done.

I awoke, rigid in terror at the raw truth that had just been exposed to me. It wasn't news to God that I believed the words I had just heard myself speak, *or* that I felt that way toward him. It had only been news to *me*. And it had been *shocking* news to me.

God had used the envelope of sleep to deliver a clear message to my now-wide-awake self: *I believed that because God hadn't completely healed me yet, that he was never going to. And I felt deeply hurt, betrayed, and angry with him about it.*

An Invitation to God

Not too long before that night, a wise Christian sister had challenged me to ask God to reveal lies to me and to replace them with the truth.[1] I had jumped at the idea. Primed by the recent experience of having my entire understanding of human existence changed when God replaced a false belief with the truth, I had eagerly invited God to reveal any other lie that might still be standing in my way.

Then came the jolting dream,[2] in which I heard, straight from my own lips, my belief that *because God hadn't healed me yet, he was never going to.* That idea, hidden so deeply within me that I hadn't even recognized it was there, had been at work: it had made me feel abandoned and far from God's care.

The Devil had used piles of circumstantial evidence—the healings I had long prayed for that hadn't come; the collection of new problems that had piled on top of the old, unresolved, ones; and God's prolonged silence—to make his case that *God just wasn't ever going to intervene for me. I was on my own.*

My Enemy had turned me—oh, so subtly—away from continuing to ask in faith for the help of the only one with the power to help me, and away from actively believing that God even *wanted* to help me.

Demolition

When the Wall Came Down

When I read in the Bible about choirs marching and singing atop the rebuilt wall of Jerusalem (Nehemiah 12:27–39), I always had trouble fathoming such a wall. In my experience, walls were narrow things, only about 6 inches thick, and hollow—made of a wood frame covered with relatively thin drywall. They served to hold up a few pictures and maybe a clock, but they were in no way constructed to support marching processionals of *people* on them.

But in China, I had walked on the Great Wall. Its stone watchtowers and fortresses gave it the feel of a building, such as a castle or fort. And standing on its open spaces was like being on the roof of a sturdy building.

When even a portion of such a consequential wall is broken down (as the walls of Jerusalem had been destroyed in Nehemiah's time, or as a significant part of the Great Wall is missing now), it's noticeable.

My shocking dream, and the revelation it contained, had been the very thing God used to tear down a large wall in my life that needed to come down. He had demolished it by simply *exposing* it. And the change was noticeable.

God let me see its rubble around me. There was its foundation, the one single lie on which the whole thing had rested: the lie that *because God hasn't completely healed me yet, he is never going to.* And there were the massive stones that had been stacked on top of the lie: *betrayal, hopelessness,* and *anger.*

Yet, until I was set free, I had not realized that I had been deceived into cooperating with my Enemy to build a wall between myself and God. I hadn't even been *aware* of the wall or of my entrapment by it, like one of those many prisoners conscripted to build the Great Wall whose bodies had ended up *inside* it.

God had liberated me from that wall. I was no longer trapped *inside* it, and no longer weighed down *under* those stones.

The absence of all of that oppression was *very* noticeable to me. I had a new and palpable sense of hope and alive-ness. I had been set free from a heavy, invisible lie. I felt lighter in every way.

I didn't consider for a moment that there might be still more lies.

4

Commissioned

Note: This chapter contains spoilers for the movie Captain Marvel.

I'm not the typical superhero movie fan. I'm married to the fan. And so, as I prepared to watch *Captain Marvel* with my husband, I said, "Okay, tell me what I need to know to not be totally lost." He concisely got me up to speed on where this tale fit into an overarching story, and how its characters related to the genre's pantheon. A couple of minutes later, I was ready to watch the movie.

And I was more than usually expectant that I would *find* something in the story.

In high school English, I was taught that every story has a protagonist and an antagonist, and that there is always some conflict between good and evil. After having lived a while, I now understand that in a new way: It's not just that every story *has* these things. It's that there is only *one* story. Every story a human can live, or imagine, is part of that story; we are all *in it*. And I was prepared to look at *this* story in that way—to see not only the small story, but also consider its relation to the larger one.

But even though I was prepared for more than what was presented on the screen, I was still surprised at what actually happened.

As the tale unfolded, we learned that the main character had been caught in an invisible web of deceit. *Up* had been made to appear *down; in* had been made to appear *out*—every lie that could have derailed her life and purpose had been engineered and employed by her enemy to do so. But then the lies began to be uncovered. And as each lie was *exposed* as a lie, its *power* was broken. With the truth, came her *freedom*.

And then she made a simple but bold proclamation to those who had worked against the truth: *She was coming to end the lies.*

And I cried. Right there in the movie theater.

I cried because I suddenly understood, in a way I couldn't yet explain, that in *my* real life, *I* had been somehow caught in a web of lies, woven so expertly by the Liar (John 8:44) that I hadn't even seen it.

But I also understood that *God was coming to end the lies—and so was I.*

I didn't yet fully know what that meant, but I knew that it was real, because it had already begun. The work of God *is* to destroy lies (1 John 3:8; John 8:44), and he had already *been* at work in my life, exposing and shattering them (2 Corinthians 10:5). I was already enjoying a new level of freedom as a result.

Apparently he was just getting started.

5

After God had awakened in me the truth that the case wasn't closed regarding my healing, I wanted to take action to build my faith *for* healing. I knew that what *I* would need in order to be healed was that thing we call a *miracle*, a *healing* right from the hand of God. Years of the best human efforts had already been tried.

When I heard about a scholarly written work that documented modern-day miracles in a serious way, I immediately got the volumes and began reading.[1] The evidence, I reasoned, would build my faith for miracles, and, in particular, for healing. "Faith comes from hearing," says Romans 10:17.

The Bible is right. Hearing (in this case, by *reading*), from a believable source, the miracles that God is doing today *did* increase my faith for healing and other miracles.

I also read testimonies of some Christians who had credibly lived *out* Jesus's words in John 14:12, "I tell you the truth, anyone who believes in me will do the same works I have done, and even greater works, because I am going to be with the Father." One of these people was Francis MacNutt, whose ministry of Christian healing and writing benefitted hundreds of thousands of people.

I had been making my way through his books for several months, when, one summer day, I finally came to *The Healing Reawakening*.[2] So much deception was exposed in the pages of that book, that I was fundamentally changed by the truth. And I was angry at the lies.

Lies and Oppression

MacNutt's book revealed how Satan has attempted, through clever means, to kill, steal, and destroy the healing ministry of the church. For thousands of years, through multiple strategies, many of which *sounded pious* (recall that Satan disguises himself as an angel of light; see 2 Corinthians 11:14), collective unbelief and lies had been shaped. I was an unwitting poster child for how far he had gotten, and so were many other unhealed people I knew. *I had been caught*—along with countless unsuspecting others—in a web of deceit.

I saw that the loss of so much of the healing ministry of Christ today *is* Satan's oppression of individuals who *could* have been healed by now. Because of Enemy oppression of the healing ministry *in the church itself*, many—perhaps including me—*haven't* been healed.

When Jesus said "the thief's purpose is to steal and kill and destroy" (John 10:10), he meant it. When Jesus came to rule "with a powerful arm" (as prophesied in Isaiah 40:10), his rule brought healing of all kinds of sickness and disease and paralysis, driving out of demons, and raising of the dead. Jesus, by those actions, was setting free the *oppressed* (see Isaiah 58:6; Luke 4:16–21; Luke 7:20–22).

Jesus had brought *the kingdom of Heaven* with him: the kingdom was at hand (Luke 10:9; Matthew 10:7). Jesus had brought *freedom from oppression* with him (Luke 4:18; Isaiah 61:1), and *healing* was a very real part of that freedom. Anyone who has ever been healed of something significant has been *freed from a very real form of oppression.*

Authority Over the Enemy

Jesus's three-year earthly ministry was a fulfillment of Isaiah 40:10—but not the *completion* of it. Jesus is not done fulfilling that prophecy on earth. His power and authority are still active here and now: Jesus *gave his followers* "authority over all the power of the enemy" (Luke 10:19).

I saw that, as the rightful agents of Christ's authority, we followers of Christ are supposed to be carrying out the *ongoing* fulfillment of Isaiah 40:10 until it is finally, fully completed at Jesus's return. We are supposed to be acting, in cooperation with God's powerful arm, to set free the oppressed *now*.

Jesus said, "I tell you the truth, anyone who believes in me will do the same works I have done, and even greater works, because I am going to be with the Father" (John 14:12). And *anyone who believes in Jesus* includes *me*.

Yet, I didn't have the first idea how to do the same works Jesus has done, and even greater works. And I knew I wasn't alone in that.

And no wonder. Because when Satan couldn't *overcome* God's power, he tried to hide it from the church—for a long, long time. He wove a thick curtain of lies—and did it so gradually, over so many countless generations, in such seemingly innocuous ways—that most of us never realized we've been tricked. We don't even *know* we've been robbed of using the authority we inherited from God.

At the time of this writing, there are over 197 million unhealed people in America alone.[3] That's 60 percent of the U.S. population. Globally, one in every three adults has more than one chronic health condition[4]—that's more than 2.5 billion people. And now I had the very strong realization that it's *really* not supposed to be this way. The church is supposed to be cooperating with God to *heal* many of those people.

The sick *are* being *oppressed* by the devil in the form of all kinds of disease and sickness—and those who believe in Jesus are supposed to be *breaking the chains of their oppression*. (See Isaiah 58:6; 61:1; Luke 4:18–21; 6:9; 13:10–16; Acts 10:38.)

Some, including Christian healing minister Agnes Sanford (1897–1982), have made the point that the only kind of suffering the Christ-follower was *meant* to endure is *religious persecution*, and that the church has been given Christ's ministry of *healing* in order to *destroy* the work of the devil in the area of health.⁵ But Satan *will* use the area of health to cause suffering, to the extent that we leave it open to him.

I realized that *one* reason that the number of unhealed is so large and still growing is that not enough Christians are carrying out the fullness of the commission Christ gave us with his authority to do the same works he has done and even greater ones (John 14:12–14).

Now that I knew that I, as a follower of Christ, was always intended to have that authority, I meant to reclaim what the Enemy had cruelly managed to keep hidden from me for too long.

I was beginning to understand God's message that *he was coming to end the lies and so was I.*

6

What Does God Want?

I now saw that, although I had always intended to have only one God, I had somehow ended up with two: God on paper and God in real life.

God *on paper* was the God who had given his word through Zechariah that, "It is a worthless shepherd who does not heal the injured" (Zechariah 11:15–17). God on paper was a God who *wanted* to heal. The New Testament is filled with healings, and in no case was the *will of God* ever cited as a reason for a believer *not* being healed.[1] (More about that in a moment.) God on paper was the Jesus of the New Testament who freely healed people, including *entire crowds* (Acts 5:16). He healed nine people *God knew* wouldn't even say *thank you* (Luke 17:11–19), and one person who may have brought his original problems on himself and who promptly began sinning as soon as he could walk again (John 5:5–15). God on paper *regularly* healed *impossible* things, including blindness and paralysis. But God in real life—in *my* life—did not act this way, and often wasn't even asked to.

There were things that I never even *thought* of God doing anything about. These were conditions I never even *thought* to call *incurable*, because, well, they were just *irrevocable*. Done. Finished. They had happened, end of story, and the person was just going to have to live with it until they died, for however long that might be, even if it was another 50 or 70 years. It never entered my mind to believe that God *might* intervene in certain cases, because I had never seen it.

I quoted, "He is the LORD, the God of all the peoples of the world. Nothing is too hard for him" (Jeremiah 32:27, author's paraphrase). But while I *thought* I was walking by faith and not by sight (2 Corinthians 5:7), my belief was *actually* approximately exactly the size of what I had seen.

Yet, for a long time, I never thought much about why God on paper and the God of my real life were so different from each other when it came to healing.

And so, when I began reading the documentation of the many contemporary healings Keener had recorded in his two-volume work *Miracles*,² the truth was quite an eye-opener. *Here*, in *real life*, was the *same* God I had met on paper, in the Bible. It turned out that God *was* still working as a healer of people, even healing things I had not known could be healed.

I wanted *that* God to be the God of my real life.

Obstacles

My unbelief had been so cleverly concealed—from myself—that it was hard to recognize. I believed that God *could* heal—and I knew that he even *sometimes did*, even though I had never personally seen a healing miracle.

But I had no firm conviction that God really *wanted* to heal in more than just a few far-flung cases, especially when prayers for healing of the more difficult things—for myself and for others—had not resulted in healing.

I've come to understand that *that* kind of belief is more accurately described as *unbelief* (see James 1:6).

Unbelief that frustrates healing miracles is not a new problem (Matthew 13:58). But even our unbelief doesn't cancel God's willingness to heal (Matthew 17:15–20; Mark 9:23–25).

In the case of a boy God *wanted* to heal, when Jesus's own disciples did not get the job done, Jesus himself identified *three* obstacles to his disciples' ability to heal the boy: unbelief (Matthew 17:20), not enough prayer (Matthew 17:21), and not enough fasting (Matthew 17:21 NKJV). None of those obstacles resided in God. And the obstacles weren't within the sick person, either.

Back when I spent years wrestling with the unmet expectation that James 5:14–16 created in me, and was studying everything I could get my hands on regarding why I wasn't *seeing* what that Scripture was *saying*, I came upon an invented explanation for the reason not everyone is healed as that Scripture states.[3] The invention went like this: *there was an added stipulation that the reader needed to bring to the text of James 5, and that was that the healing had to also be the will of God.* In other words, as that view goes, James's writing in Scripture that clearly states believers will be healed—physically as well as spiritually—in response to a certain type of prayer by certain persons *is not inherently clearly indicative of the primary, general will of God to heal.*

The invented explanation didn't sit quite right in my spirit, but I couldn't say why at the time. *Didn't it have to be true? Otherwise, why wouldn't God be getting his way and more people be getting healed?*

However, as I read Francis MacNutt's book *The Healing Reawakening*, I found out *why* that invented idea hadn't been sitting right in my spirit: It was based on the false premise that *it is not generally God's will to heal people.* And the direct result of *that* lie has been *unbelief.*

For generations, some religious people had tried to get rid of an inconvenient discrepancy between what Scripture *says* and what they *saw*—by embracing an untrue explanation for the disparity: the idea that in many—or even most—cases, *it was no longer God's will to heal.*

But the explanation was *not* based on Scripture. God hasn't changed his mind about his general will to heal people.

A God Who Wants To Heal

From beginning to end, Scripture reveals a God who generally[4] always *wants* to heal, even when there are factors that delay or block the healing:

- When God spoke to the Israelites just three days after bringing them out of Egypt, he told them he was "the LORD who heals you" (Exodus 15:26). Healing is an integral part of his identity.
- In the Old Testament, God revealed health as central to his desire for his people (Exodus 23:25; Isaiah 53:5; Jeremiah 17:14; 30:17; 33:6). King David knew God as *the one who heals "all my diseases"* (Psalm 103:3).
- Both the scope and the success rate of the incarnate Jesus's healing ministry, as recorded in the Gospels (Matthew, Mark, Luke, and John), indicate the *pervasiveness* of God's will to heal. Jesus healed *entire crowds*. He healed people who came to him or were brought to him for healing—and even some who were too sick to come to him (Matthew 4:24; 8:5–13, 16; 9:20–22; 12:15; 14:35–36; 17:17–18; Mark 5:22–23, 35–43; 6:56; Luke 4:40; 5:15; 8:26–39; Acts 5:16).
- When asked, Jesus compassionately affirmed the will of God to heal (Mark 1:41; Luke 5:13).

- Jesus affirmed the will of God to heal even when healing was delayed, either necessarily[5] or unnecessarily (Acts 3:2–8; Luke 13:10–13; John 9:1, 3; 11:14–15).[6]
- Jesus affirmed the will of God to heal, even when his own disciples had been unable to carry out God's will because they had not prayed and fasted enough and did not have the necessary faith to be the agents of the healing (Mark 9:17–29; Matthew 17:14–21; Luke 9:37–42).
- Jesus made a direct statement (recorded in John 14:12) that believers in him would do even greater things than the works he did, indicating that he *intended* for widespread healing—done by his authority and through God's power—to continue.
- Isaiah prophesied that we would be healed by Jesus's *wounds* (Isaiah 53:5).
- God confirmed the truth of the message of salvation by granting signs and wonders, including healing, to be done by those sharing his message (Mark 16:20; Acts 4:29–30; 6:8; 8:6; 14:3; Hebrews 2:4). God made signs and wonders part of fully sharing the good news (Romans 15:18–19).
- Scripture also indicates that God gives spiritual gifts of healing to be used to care for the church (1 Corinthians 12:9, 25), a body which suffers when even one member suffers (1 Corinthians 12:26).

Paul's Thorn and God's Will

Even Paul's thorn in the flesh is *not* proof that it was not the will of God to heal Paul.

Paul had been given specific revelation as to why this particular weakness had been *given*, as well as revelation about how God would meet Paul's needs *while* he lived with this torment, but God *never* said it was *not his will* to remove it (2 Corinthians 12:7–9).[7]

I believe it is likely that God eagerly waited for the day that Paul *could* safely be delivered from his thorn without succumbing to pride.

What Does It Matter?

Some might be thinking, *If God hasn't healed me (or my loved one)—regardless of the reason—then what does it even matter whether he generally wants to heal or not?*

To that, my answer is that *it makes a great difference*. For one thing, it matters greatly to the faith of a sick person—and to their entire relationship with God—when they erroneously believe that the God who is supposed to *love* them doesn't *want* to *heal* them.

It also makes a difference to those *through* whom God desires to heal, so that they will actively cooperate with God in accomplishing his will.

It is of vital importance to the faith of the *entire body of Christ* to know that Scripture reveals a God who *does* want to heal.

Why Aren't More People Being Healed?

If God generally always *wants* to heal, then why is *every* sick person not healed—or at least a great many more than *are* being healed?

One reason some people are not healed, and I think it's a big one, is that *God's will is not always done on earth.*[8]

The truth of this point is chiefly made by Jesus, who taught his disciples to *pray for God's will to be done on earth as it is in Heaven* (Matthew 6:9–10). There would be no need at all to pray such a prayer if God's will *were* always automatically done. As it turns out, however, there are a *number* of obstacles to God's will being done on earth—in all kinds of matters, not just healing.

Choosing Sides

Because God's will is *not* always being done in every single matter on earth, Jesus also taught his followers to pray to be *delivered* from evil.

There is a very real conflict in this world between good and evil, with its source in the spiritual realm (Ephesians 6:12). Daniel's story provides insight about rebellious supernatural interference with God's will being carried out (see Daniel 10:12–14). It was God's *will* to grant Daniel understanding in response to Daniel's prayers. But the holy supernatural messenger bringing God's answer to Daniel was delayed for 21 days because of a struggle with an evil supernatural opponent. God's forces *did* eventually prevail in the struggle in the heavenly realms, and Daniel finally received the answer he had sought from God. But God's *will* was never at issue during that weeks-long struggle. The problem was *active spiritual opposition to the enacting of God's will*.

Humans also participate in the conflict between good and evil. Human free will means countless opportunities each day for every person to align with either God or evil.

Consider King Saul. He became a dramatic and tragic example of someone who repeatedly chose *not* to do God's will, ✓ to the point that he became God's enemy (see 1 Samuel 15; 16:14; 1 Chronicles 10:13–14).

However, God's children can choose to *cooperate* with God to *bring about* his will. We are intended to be part of the *powerful forces of God's kingdom* for good. Believers have been given the Holy Spirit (Acts 2:17), spiritual gifts (1 Corinthians 12), and authority (Luke 10:19) *to be the agents of God's will*.

In some cases, however, God's will may not be done because God's human children have failed, for some reason other than direct rebellion, to carry out the part of it for which we bear responsibility. For example, I realized that I had been largely inactive in the area of healing ministry to others for decades of my Christian life, because of ignorance. I had lacked *awareness* of the role I was expected by God to serve in it, and I didn't understand the *importance* of acting. Yet, it is God's explicitly stated will (John 14:12) for *whoever* believes in Jesus to do the works he did and greater—to demonstrate the power of God and destroy the works of the devil (1 John 3:8).

My wrong belief—held for far too long—that *whatever happened must have been God's will* and that *my prayers for the healing of others had only minimal impact on changing the course of events, because God was probably going to do what he was going to do anyway* (and why was I even praying, again?)—was one of those seemingly innocuous, yet completely wrong, patterns of thinking that held me back for far too long from being the type of effective disciple that Jesus described in John 14:12.

A Vicious Cycle of Nothing

As I read *The Healing Reawakening* by Francis MacNutt, I saw clearly—for the first time in my life—how the church had been caught for too long in a web of lies about the healing ministry of Christ, which had led to dwindling of the healing ministry itself.

Christians became ensnared in a vicious cycle of expecting only what we have seen happen—which, for many of us, is *not much at all*. That state of affairs served to feed our expectations that *more* nothing-much would happen when we tried to minister healing. On this starvation diet, our faith for healing shriveled.

It's not God's will became such a convenient peg on which to hang unanswered (and even un-prayed) prayers for healing, that we lost our way to becoming "those who believe" described in Mark 16:17–18 (NKJV): "These signs will follow those who believe: In My name ... they will lay hands on the sick, and they will recover."

No more.

Maybe we have been *unaware* of God's overwhelming desire to heal people today and his power to do it today. Maybe we haven't *understood* the gravity of our calling to minister healing, or *known how* to live it out in daily life. Or maybe we *are trying* to cooperate with God in all of this, but are not succeeding for some reason.[9]

But let's not give up.

2 Timothy 3:16–17 says, "All Scripture is inspired by God and is useful to teach us what is true and to make us realize what is wrong in our lives. It corrects us when we are wrong and teaches us to do what is right. God uses it to prepare and equip his people to do every good work."

Let us consider how we can fulfill *all* of the qualifications of pray-ers as noted in James 5, so that we *can* carry out our God-given task *effectively*.

If there were ever an area where the believer needs to be *prepared and equipped to do every good work*, it's the healing ministry of Christ. Since James 5 is Scripture inspired by God, we must be able to profit from its teaching, correction, preparation, and equipping. So I am not eager to give myself—or the rest of the church—a pass on this one. Let's let James 5 and the rest of Scripture say what it says, and let's take it to heart.

If we take an honest look at the conditions of James 5:14–16, and ask why we are not seeing more healings arise from believers' prayers, including our own, I think we can arrive at one possibility directly from the Scripture: *as those praying for the sick, we have not yet fulfilled the instructions and conditions outlined there.*

Before you say, *God wouldn't allow the failure of well-meaning believers to prevent another person's healing*, re-read Matthew 17:14–20 and Mark 9:17–29. We know from Jesus's own mouth that there *are* times when it *is* God's will to heal, but it is the *spiritual state of the believers* who are trying to be the conduits of healing that is the obstacle to the healing God wants to give.

There is spiritual opposition to healing in this world, and it takes something *real* to overcome that opposition. The authority and power of Jesus can overcome spiritual opposition, but there is <u>a *way* for us to cooperate with Jesus</u> so that God's healing power *can* be applied; and there is also a way that *doesn't* work—as Jesus's first disciples learned in the account mentioned above. We, too, need to <u>learn how to cooperate with Jesus</u> in carrying out his healing ministry today (John 14:12).

The disciples asked the right question when they asked Jesus, *Why were we not able to heal him?* (Matthew 17:19, author's paraphrase, emphasis added). Jesus gave them a concrete answer. He didn't say, *It wasn't God's will.* He didn't say, *I didn't intend for you to do it; I will do it myself when I want it done.* He didn't say, *Don't worry about it; you wouldn't understand.* There was a very real reason that the disciples hadn't been able to heal that particular boy, even though God clearly *willed* to heal the child *and* had the *power* to heal him (Matthew 17:16–18)—and these same disciples had performed many *other* healings. And now that the disciples knew why they hadn't been able to heal the boy, they could take action. They could make themselves better prepared to minister God's healing next time.

If we *do* the things the Bible says, we can *believe* for what it promises. However, if we are not fully doing *our* part, then we are not done. We still need to grow in our cooperation with God according to his leading in this area. We need to grow in our love and compassion for our sick sisters and brothers in need of *healing ministry that heals*—and for an unsaved world that needs to know *there is really power in the name of Jesus, and this is not all just "a lot of talk"* (1 Corinthians 4:20).

I, for one, do not want to miss out—for any reason—on doing all of those things that God has prepared in advance for me to do! (Ephesians 2:10).

How Far Can We Go?

Will *everyone* be healed in *this* life? Until God's kingdom *fully* comes to earth, I believe the answer is, by definition, *no*.[10] But we are *supposed to be working in cooperation with God* to *bring* his kingdom to earth (Matthew 6:9–10; Luke 10:9; see also Matthew 24:14).

Therefore, there is a lot of ground that believers can partner with God to take between the current state of things (in which 6 of every 10 people in this country, and 1 of every 3 worldwide, live perpetually unhealed) and seeing the full number of people who absolutely *could be healed by God* in this generation, *be* healed in our lifetimes. The fact that *everyone* cannot be healed until God's kingdom fully comes, does not mean that *many more people* cannot—and should not—be healed now.

Consider the first generation of the church. *Many* people were healed through God's gift to Paul. In fact, God gave such miraculous power to Paul that even pieces of cloth Paul had *touched* carried God's healing power to sick people.

> *When handkerchiefs or aprons that had merely touched his skin were placed on sick people, they were healed of their diseases, and evil spirits were expelled.*
> ACTS 19:12

Yet, even with such miraculous power working *in him* (Colossians 1:29), Paul was once notably waylaid on a mission trip *by his own sickness* (Galatians 4:12–15). And Paul wasn't the only one. Paul once found it necessary to leave his co-laborer Trophimus *sick* at Miletus (2 Timothy 4:20). And another of Paul's co-workers, Epaphroditus (Philippians 2:25–27), also did not receive immediate healing of physical sickness—and almost died.

But Paul didn't give up on healing when *everyone* was not *immediately* healed, because Paul knew something about *fully presenting the Good News* that, for far too many generations, we have lost.

Fully Presenting the Good News

Undoubtedly, healing *is* a demonstration of God's compassion (see Matthew 9:36; 14:14) and *God cares deeply* about healing of individuals (see Luke 13:10–16; Luke 14:3–5).

But God's power revealed through healing does more than relieve an individual person's bodily suffering. Healing is not solely for the sake of healing, or so that people can just get back to the life they had in progress before sickness.

Displays of God's power through healing are *also* about fully presenting the Good News, which results in expanding the kingdom of God (see 1 Corinthians 4:20). Ultimately, healing may be given by God so that people will know God.

Paul put it concisely when he wrote, "They were convinced by the power of miraculous signs and wonders and by the power of God's Spirit. In this way, I have fully presented the Good News of Christ all the way from Jerusalem to Illyricum" (Romans 15:18–19)."

Jesus envisioned believers in him *continuing to cooperate with him in that work*—as he had been doing it—as in, "whatever you request along the lines of who *I* am and what *I* am doing, I'll do it" (John 14:13, author's paraphrase). Jesus is not at my beck and call. *I am at his, to do his work*—the work of cooperating with him as he brings his kingdom to earth (Matthew 10:7; Luke 10:9; see also Matthew 6:10).

As I look at Jesus's words in John 14:11–14 in the larger context in which he spoke them, the meaning of this passage comes to me in a fuller, truer sense: Jesus was handing off the *same work he had been doing*. He had been *bringing God's kingdom to earth*, and he intended to *continue* bringing it—*through* those who believe in him.

It is up to me to cooperate with God[12] in the ministry Jesus has already given believers to bring God's kingdom to earth *in far greater measure*—to the degree that really is possible if believers will grow into effectively carrying out healing ministry to each other in the power of God's Spirit *the way the Gospels indicate we can*. Faith is believing that God will do what Scripture says he will do.

> *"Just believe that I am in the Father and the Father is in me. Or at least believe because of the work you have seen me do.*
>
> *"I tell you the truth, anyone who believes in me will do the same works I*

have done, and even greater works, because I am going to be with the Father. You can ask for anything in my name, and I will do it, so that the Son can bring glory to the Father. Yes, ask me for anything in my name, and I will do it!"

JOHN 14:11–14

Until I see God *doing* what Scripture says he *will* do, I must speak to him honestly and with humility about the apparent discrepancy. I need to ask him to *reveal* to me *my* part in closing the gap between what Scripture *says* and what I am actually experiencing—and then ask him to *help me do my part.*

If I *believe* the Word of God—and I do—what other choice do I have but to continue to *pursue* the kind of life and faith and prayer that will result in God's healing more people—healing that will reveal his power and the reality of his kingdom?

And why would I not want to?

7

Case Not Closed

Several years ago I read a pastoral training book that advised spiritual shepherds to encourage the sick people in their care by telling them that either they'd get better soon, or they'd die and go to Heaven soon—but relief was coming soon, either way. In addition to the advice being sadly empty of participation in the healing ministry of Christ on earth, I was surprised that an experienced pastor so entirely missed the reality of the many millions of people living with life-altering chronic health conditions.

For many unhealed people, relief is *not* in view soon—perhaps not for several more decades—unless God's healing is ministered to them in a way they haven't yet encountered. The person with chronic infirmity may struggle to fit her or his faith into the conventions of thought shaped in a *get-well-soon* society.

Healed versus *not-healed* is a binary distinction, a completely *either/or* categorization. Yet, inside a life with an unhealed physical condition, a person may experience significant degrees of relief from one or more troubling symptoms—and be truly grateful for any measure of healing. But as long as healing is still needed for *other* things, the person is still in need of healing. The individual is still *unhealed*, in the binary sense.

Binary thinking about healing affects how we approach prayer for ourselves and others, and how we gauge prayer's effectiveness. This is especially true when some longstanding or complex health condition has not yet been totally healed, despite years of prayer.

In my own case, binary thinking about healing had produced a strange effect on my faith. After a number of years of prayer for healing of chronic health issues—and experiencing real relief and reversal of several symptoms, yet not others—I both *still believed that I could be completely healed and was actively seeking God and receiving prayer for that healing,* and—as my dream had revealed—*also believed, in some part of me, that God would not completely heal me because he had not already done so.*

After God gave me the incredible gift of revealing my *unbelief* to me, he gave me something to help renew my faith and energies to pray for the healing of chronic physical conditions—for myself and for others. He helped me understand that just because someone wasn't *immediately* healed by healing prayer, or didn't even *get well soon,* didn't mean they couldn't get well ever.

Through a discussion in Francis MacNutt's book *The Power to Heal,* God replaced my mistaken assumption that healing *had to occur all at once,* just as it usually had in the Bible, or that it wasn't going to happen at all. And God refuted the lie that *my* case had been closed and he was not going to heal me: <u>He had never said that.</u>

Gradual Healing and Spiritual Power

Through MacNutt's writing, God taught me that persistent prayer over months and years (MacNutt called <u>it *soaking prayer*</u>) <u>can be effective in gradual healing</u>.[1] Even though I know of no one who would not prefer an instant healing, I was heartened to know that MacNutt had seen healing of very difficult conditions through this type of <u>persistent prayer</u>.

MacNutt explained that in his decades of healing ministry, he saw that <u>it takes *a different degree of spiritual power* to heal some things, compared to others</u>. He plainly stated that some chronic illnesses are difficult to heal. That doesn't mean that God doesn't *want* to do it, or that it's not possible.

I appreciated MacNutt's forthright discussion of *why* some healings take so much longer than the speed at which Jesus healed people. <u>James 5:16 indicates that all Christians have the capacity</u> to pray *effectively* for the healing of others. However, MacNutt explained that <u>not all prayers for healing *are equally effective*</u>, and he discussed some of the reasons for the variances in outcomes.

A Man Named Ananias

One of those reasons, acknowledged by MacNutt and also taught by Agnes Sanford, is that one particular individual may not be the right person to pray for other particular individuals.

In her writings and talks on Christian healing, Sanford referred to seeking the Lord's guidance *before* praying for another person, in order to know if that person was "in her bundle," as she called it. People in her bundle were those for whom the Lord wanted *her* to pray for healing. She was clear on the fact that if a person were not in her bundle, she was not the one to pray.

Conversely, if she knew she *was* to pray for the healing of a certain person—either because she had asked the Father who she should pray for, and he had told her; or she had asked the Father if she were to pray for a certain person, and he had responded affirmatively—she was then able to pray *the prayer of faith* for that person to be healed.

She never mixed *prayers for guidance* in this matter with *prayers for healing*, because, as she wisely pointed out, the result of such mixture in the same prayer was *not a prayer of faith* for the healing of the sick person.[2]

It is interesting to consider the relationship between that teaching and Jesus's statement that he could do only what he saw the Father doing (John 5:19). As critics of Jesus as healer are fond of pointing out, even *he* did not heal *everyone* who was sick at the time he walked the earth. Those critics have unwittingly helped me to understand this point very clearly: God did not *intend* for Jesus to heal every sick person who was alive while he was incarnate (see Luke 4:42–43).³ God does not expect *me* to heal every sick person alive today, or *you* to, either. God expects each part of the body to do part of the work, but no one part of the body to do all of the work. Each believer will have his or her own assignments. It will be *wisdom* for us to obtain guidance from God as to what *our* individual assignments are (and then, of course, *obedience* and *life* for us to do them; see John 4:34).

Presumably, there were a number of Holy Spirit-empowered Christ-followers *in* Damascus,⁴ any one of whom God could have called upon to lay hands on Saul. However, from among all of them, God chose Ananias for the task (Acts 9:10–18). When Ananias obeyed the Lord and laid hands on Saul, Saul regained his vision and was filled with the Holy Spirit, and was baptized (Acts 9:17–18).

More Power

MacNutt's writing in *The Power to Heal* helped me see another reason that not all prayers for the sick are equally effective: the spiritual power of those *praying* varies. MacNutt compassionately discussed how individuals can *increase the effectiveness of our prayers* by cooperating with *the increase of the life of Christ* in our own lives.

Mountain Moving and Effective Praying

God used Francis MacNutt's testimony to help *renew* my faith for my own healing.

But it was also a wake-up call. MacNutt's teaching was a catalyst for making me want to increase my life in Christ so that I can *be* a more effective conduit of the kind of healing that those in *my* bundle need.

I am moved by compassion to want to be able to carry out what Jesus expects me to be able to do in terms of healing others. I don't want someone God desires to heal to remain unhealed because I haven't fully done *my* part in the body of Christ (see Mark 9:14–29).

I'm not there yet. I'm learning. I'm trying. So far, most of the people I have ministered to would be able to say to Jesus the same thing the man in Matthew 17:16 said to Jesus: *your disciple couldn't heal*. The situation wasn't acceptable to Jesus then, and I can't think it's good enough for him now. It's not sitting well with me, either. James 5 sets the bar for Christ-followers in a certain place when it comes to the healing of our Christian sisters and brothers. Scripture expects that we will see them *be healed!*

So what do I do about it?

Several Christians have written on the reality of what happens in the physical world when Christians engage faith and prayer.[5] The mechanisms and principles by which faith and prayer work are not imaginary, but are actual.

When Jesus talked about our ability to move mountains by faith, and to receive whatever we ask for in accordance with God's will (see Matthew 21:21; 1 John 5:14), he was talking about something *real*, and something that is supposed to be central to the life of his disciples.

I have a huge opportunity here for growth as a disciple of Christ. I am moving mountains much more slowly than I would like—in fact, imperceptibly, if at all. My prayers are less effective than I would like—*and than Scripture indicates they can be*!

But I now understand that my *capacity* to move mountains and to pray effectively is not fixed. *It can grow.*

And it needs to!

8

Seeing the Battlefield

I think that part of the urgency I feel to become a more effective disciple of Christ is that a curtain has been pulled back revealing the conflict between God's kingdom and the kingdom of darkness.

It took a long time for me to recognize that spiritual warfare of the kind that Paul described in Ephesians isn't the occasional *exception* in the believer's life. It is the *rule*. It has *been* the rule for a long time (see 2 Kings 6:8–23):

> *For we are not fighting against flesh-and-blood enemies, but against evil rulers and authorities of the unseen world, against mighty powers in this dark world, and against evil spirits in the heavenly places.*
> EPHESIANS 6:12

If the Enemy was hoping to keep me in dark in this matter, his overdone approach has betrayed him. I now understand that I have long been in *his* attentions, but now *he* has come directly to mine. I have finally realized in an undeniable way that there is a *real war* going on between two spiritual kingdoms, and I am *in* it.

I've also realized that attempting to solve certain problems in the physical realm is an illusion, because they have their roots in the *spiritual* world. And so, when I bring *natural* solutions to *supernaturally caused* problems, they are either unsolvable in that manner, or as soon as one problem goes away, two more take its place. I won't win my battles by charging directly at what *appear* to be the issues in the *physical* realm.

But I *can* win.

The first step to victory is knowing my God-given identity and role.

Going On the Offensive

God has shown me who I am in this war, and it is not at all who Satan suggested I was.

God has shown me that I am not an unprotected *object of attack* in this spiritual war. Satan wanted me to think so, but that is a *lie*. I am *not* unnamed cannon fodder.

I am also not an *infant*, fit only to be snatched from danger and whisked from this world to the next as quickly as possible. Satan wanted me to think so, but that, too, is a *lie*. God intends me to be mature (see Hebrews 5:13; 1 Corinthians 3:1–2). I *was* a spiritual infant at one time, but now is not that time.

Satan wanted me to believe that I was *powerless*. But God has also shown me that that is a lie. Not only do I already have spiritual power, God has shown me ways to increase it.

I have been designated to *fight*—not only to defend, but also to *go on the offensive* to bring the kingdom of God to earth. I have been given spiritual weapons to demolish strongholds:

> For the weapons of our warfare are not carnal but mighty in God for pulling down strongholds, casting down arguments and every high thing that exalts itself against the knowledge of God, bringing every thought into captivity to the obedience of Christ...
> 2 CORINTHIANS 10:4–5 (NKJV)

Weapons of Warfare

God showed me five instruments I would need for my assignment. He taught me about using *forgiveness*—for gaining freedom; *faith*—for protection; *prayer*—to bring God's will on earth; *God's Word*—to destroy lies; and *my words*—to bring life.

These were all truths that had long been in plain view in Scripture, but that he now made real to me in a deeper way. They would be vital to my spiritual arsenal for gaining victory "against evil rulers and authorities of the unseen world, against mighty powers in this dark world, and against evil spirits in the heavenly places" (Ephesians 6:12).

The Route of Forgiveness

Jesus loved to use stories when he taught. The accounts of his teachings in the Gospels are filled with them.

One night, God used a story to teach me the potential of *forgiveness*. The story was told to me in a dream (see Acts 2:17).

In an old library with very high ceilings and rows and rows of tall wooden bookcases, I was being chased by demons. They appeared in the form of large, menacing animals with scaly hide, dinosaur-like tails, and bared teeth. Between the library shelves and around them we ran—me, ahead of them, moving as fast as I could; and all of them closing the distance behind me.

Within the dream, as I continued to barely outrun the evil entities, I was urged by God's Spirit to forgive certain persons (people I know and had forgiven in my waking life). In the dream, I immediately forgave those people as I continued to run, and something *immediately* changed. I was suddenly able to move freely on a plane far above where the demons could reach. While they were all still limited to running on the floor, between and around the bookshelves, I now had a way available to me *above* the floor that they had no means at all of accessing.

Using the new way, I immediately moved to an exit at the corner of the room, and passed through it into a stairwell, from which I was able to leave the building entirely. Outside, in the sunshine, I was safe. The creatures were no longer behind me, and I soon realized they wouldn't be coming at all. They *couldn't* reach me there.

The message of the dream had not been about how *good* and *nice* it is to forgive. It had been a stark lesson about the *necessity* of, and *spiritual potential* proceeding from, forgiveness. Forgiveness was the difference between being caught by, or being free from, the Enemy.

Faith Shield

God also showed me how my faith is a conduit and container of his power for my protection.

> And *through your faith, God is protecting you by his power* until you receive this salvation, which is ready to be revealed on the last day for all to see.
>
> 1 PETER 1:5

God's power surges into my *faith* to shield me every day until the last day, protecting my *spirit* from the evil that *would destroy it* on this earth *unless* God did protect it by his power.[1]

It is the same kind of protection that Paul referred to in 2 Timothy 4:18, when he—who had suffered physically in many ways—wrote, "The Lord will deliver me from every evil attack and will bring me safely into his heavenly Kingdom." *All* that had been done to Paul had been done *to the body*. But God had protected his *soul* (Matthew 10:28). That's not a consolation prize.

It's a beautiful, shining miracle that stirs me to awe and thanksgiving every time I can catch a glimpse of its meaning.

My own faith is the very real conduit of God's power to protect me in this vital way.² Knowing that my faith is *that* important encourages me to *increase* it.

Prayer in Bowls

When I was growing up, a Bible verse hung on a wall in my home. It was 1 Thessalonians 5:17 (NKJV), "pray without ceasing." Although I didn't understand then how it would be possible to actually *do* the thing that it said, the injunction was embedded deeply in me. (I understand it a little more now, since God has clearly revealed to me that some part of me can pray to him while I am asleep, unrestrained by waking inhibitions.)

Why was this so important, I wondered? Wasn't prayer just *words*? Didn't God only consider the *message* the words had conveyed, while the *form* of the prayer itself just vanished like a mist?

Apparently not.

I don't think I ever realized how much substance prayer actually has until I considered two Scriptures. In Revelation 5:8, I saw the reality of the existence of the saints' prayers—in another form—in Heaven. And in Mark 9:29 (see also Matthew 17:21), Jesus named the disciples' lack of *prayer* (along with their lack of fasting and faith) as a reason for their failure—apparently their *first* failure—at healing.

Scripture reveals that prayer isn't just some vanishing, *nothing* kind of thing. It is a *real* thing. Prayer *becomes incense* in bowls in Heaven; it becomes *a useful article of substance*, stored in the presence of the Lamb himself (Revelation 5:8). Prayers so stored can be poured out by angels in Heaven as an offering to God (Revelation 8:3–4)—and not only at some distant time in the future, but during the lifetime of the one praying (Acts 10:4).

Scripture also reveals that prayer is a thing with *continued existence*—a thing that, having been done *previously*, can result in one's being spiritually prepared *today* to bring about God's will on earth—such as by healing a child who presents with an urgent need (see Mark 9:25–29).

I began to see prayer in a whole new way.

And so, when I began to learn more about certain kinds of Christian prayer, including spiritual protection prayer, spiritual warfare prayer,[3] and others, I was prepared by my new appreciation of the *substance* of prayer—and by my own urgent need in spiritual warfare—to approach them seriously. As I began to pray these kinds of prayers, I saw that they were both effective and necessary in spiritual battle.

> *Pray in the Spirit at all times and on every occasion. Stay alert and be persistent in your prayers for all believers everywhere.*
> EPHESIANS 6:18

Words as Weapons

When Ephesians 6:17 (NKJV) calls the *Word of God* the *Sword of the Spirit*, it is *not* merely a poetic symbol. The Word of God is a real weapon in the spiritual realm, both as a tool for creation and for destruction.

God created this world by speaking words *through* the Word who became flesh, Jesus (see Genesis 1; John 1:1–5, 14).

Hebrews 4:12 describes the power and precision of the speech of God to act in us individually for our ultimate spiritual benefit: "For the word of God is living and powerful, and sharper than any two-edged sword, piercing even to the division of soul and spirit, and of joints and marrow, and is a discerner of the thoughts and intents of the heart" (NKJV).

When Jesus was tempted by Satan in the wilderness, he *destroyed* the work of the devil *with words from Scripture* (see Matthew 4:1–11; Luke 4:1–13). We, also, can use God's Word to destroy the Enemy's work, just as 2 Corinthians 10:4–5 says.

God has also designed this world such that the words of *all humans*—even the wicked—wield power, to the degree he has determined (see Proverbs 11:11). Words heard and read, Words spoken and written (see Proverbs 4:23–24).

My own words are weapons to bring about life and death (see Proverbs 18:21).

And so, to my love for the Word, God added the knowledge that *I was to use God's Word as Jesus had* used it in the wilderness—head-on, to destroy the work of Satan.

And to my love of writing, God added the revelation that he was forming with it *a specific spiritual weapon*.

> *We faithfully preach the truth. God's power is working in us. We use the weapons of righteousness in the right hand for attack and the left hand for defense.*
> 2 CORINTHIANS 6:7

9

Active Duty

God seemed to be training and preparing me—even while I slept.

But a significant obstacle appeared to still be in the way of my life: my own unhealed body.

An assumption had crept into my thinking long ago that *first* God would heal me, and *then* I could get on with his work. While I could do some things without being completely healed—and those things I faithfully did—I still had the idea that I was prevented from *really* getting on with the fullest expression of what he had made me for.

And then, in a gradual work of the Holy Spirit, one day I started thinking about Paul, writing large chunks of what became the New Testament—*while incarcerated*. And I thought about John, seeing the Revelation of Christ and writing it down in a book—*while exiled on Patmos*.

I thought about Romans 11:29: "For God's gifts and his call can never be withdrawn." And Philippians 1:6: "And I am certain that God, who began the good work within you, will continue his work until it is finally finished on the day when Christ Jesus returns."

I realized that it was a *lie* that I would be excluded from the work of the kingdom *until* I could pass some sort of physical.

I was riveted by these words from Paul's letter to the Galatians:

You were well aware that the reason I ended up preaching to you was that I was physically broken, and so, prevented from continuing on my journey, I was forced to stop with you. That is how I came to preach to you.
GALATIANS 4:12–13 (MSG)

Isn't that where I am, too?

The hard parts of Paul's life are not the stuff that my dreams are made of. Yet, even though Paul's health was broken and his personal freedom severely limited, I have never heard anyone breathe a word to the effect that Paul's life may not have been *enough*, or that even while he spent time *imprisoned* or *unhealed*, he lived a *less-than* existence. The thought simply doesn't occur. And I think there's a good reason for that.

Whatever his situation—and there were some doozies—Paul continued to work for the kingdom of God. He composed letters to the churches for their instruction, encouragement, and growth. Those letters would become part of the Scriptures and would be instrumental in building the global church for generations. Paul's labor during his most difficult times had an outcome like the blowing of seed from a plant: It served to spread the good news of Christ, around the world and into many future seasons.

Keeping On

Paul had been assigned a responsibility, and had been spiritually equipped by God to carry out his task (Acts 9:15; 19:11–12; Ephesians 3:2; 4:11–12).

And then Paul kept on. His life was *full* of hard things (2 Corinthians 11:23–28), none of which he allowed to stop his fruitful work for the kingdom. He focused on using whatever God gave him (John 3:27; 2 Corinthians 3:5) to do the work of God. Even Paul's request for prayer demonstrated his focus on *continuing the work* that had been assigned to him:

> *And pray for me, too. Ask God to give me the right words so I can boldly explain God's mysterious plan that the Good News is for Jews and Gentiles alike. I am in chains now, still preaching this message as God's ambassador. So pray that I will keep on speaking boldly for him, as I should.*
> EPHESIANS 6:19–20

And Paul told the church to use his life as an example of how to live:

> *Keep putting into practice all you learned and received from me— everything you heard from me and saw me doing. Then the God of*

peace will be with you.
PHILLIPIANS 4:9

Paul never entertained the idea that his *circumstances* should be permitted to make his work for God's kingdom less fruitful. *So, what if I don't, either?*

John didn't. His circumstances were not permitted by God to take him out of action in God's kingdom. Even though John was a prisoner on an island, physically separated from the seven local churches to whom he wrote,[1] he was still a *brother* and *partner* to others in the kingdom (Revelation 1:9). Christ had a message for *all* of them, and John was writing it down in a book for them (see Revelation 1:11). In it, Christ let his siblings know that God *saw* their difficult circumstances, and that *they still had specific things to do within the kingdom.*[2]

The memoir of Nehemiah is a testament to God's people *building* with one hand, while *defending against evil opposition* with the other (see Nehemiah 1–7, especially 4:16–18).

God is not stopped by difficult circumstances (2 Timothy 2:8). Even when things happen that are *not* his will, *he makes them yield good* (Romans 8:28; Job 42:2).

So, what if I refuse to wait for *my* circumstances to improve? What if I decide that, *even while persistently pursuing healing from God—with faith that he wants me to be healed,* I will press on with living his will for my life?

Make it so.

So, then, I thought, *what do I need in order to get on with the work that was assigned to my life long before I was born, by the God who saw everything coming that has come* (Psalm 139:16)?

10

Power

That's why I work and struggle so hard, depending on Christ's mighty power that works within me.

COLOSSIANS 1:29

Paul expected all believers to have Christ's mighty power working within *them* the way it worked within *him* (see 1 Corinthians 11:1; Romans 8:11; Ephesians 1:19–21).

And so did Jesus:

I tell you the truth, anyone who believes in me will do the same works I have done, and even greater works, because I am going to be with the Father.

JOHN 14:12

It doesn't take much of a gap analysis to figure out that I'm missing something. I am *not* aware of the level of Christ's power working within *me* that Paul consistently depended on within *him*.

For too long I had believed that everything that happened in matters of sickness and healing had already been filtered through

God's will. In this view of things, I was mostly rendered something like a compassionate bystander. *And I was wrong!*

Now, he has made me understand that being part of the body of Christ <u>means *acting as his body*</u>. He has commissioned believers to take specific action on his behalf (see Mark 16:15–18). I am meant to be one of the people through whom God's power is working today, to bring about his will, and therefore, his kingdom, on earth—where his will is *not* always done and where my life—my prayers, actions, and words—are influential factors in outcomes.

So *how* would I do these things that Jesus said *anyone who believes in him* would do (John 14:12)? How would I get from where I was to this state of being that Jesus labeled as *"the truth"* (John 14:12)?

Fish, Eggs, and the Holy Spirit

In Luke 11:1–13, <u>Jesus gives a teaching on prayer</u>, which concludes this way:

> *"You fathers—if your children ask for a fish, do you give them a snake instead? Or if they ask for an egg, do you give them a scorpion? Of course not! So if you sinful people know how to give good gifts to your children, how much more will your heavenly Father give the Holy Spirit to those who ask him."*
>
> LUKE 11:11–13

I thought I understood the part about the fish and the egg, but after that, the story seemed to go off the rails. Wasn't Jesus talking about things we *didn't have* and *needed from God?* Why was *asking the Father to give the Holy Spirit* the conclusion to a teaching of Jesus on *persistent audacity in prayer?*

I knew from Scripture that the Holy Spirit worked in many ways in the life of the believer (Romans 8:26)—including sealing us (Ephesians 1:13; Revelation 7:3), teaching us and reminding us of Christ's teaching (John 14:26), guiding us (Galatians 5:16, 25, John 16:13), telling us about the future (John 16:13), praying for us (Romans 8:26–27), giving us spiritual gifts (1 Corinthians 12:4, 11), producing fruit (Galatians 5:22–23), and filling us with power (Luke 24:49).

But I'd always assumed that the Holy Spirit did as much of that as he wanted to once he had initially been invited into my life. Was Jesus saying there was *more* of the Holy Spirit to ask for, seek, and knock after (Luke 11:9–10)?

As I dug into the Scriptures regarding the Holy Spirit, I noticed that the working of God's Spirit *really* cannot be put into a box. Eleven of the disciples received the Spirit when Jesus breathed on them (John 20:22) and then later those same eleven also were filled with *power when the Holy Spirit came on them* (Luke 24:49; Acts 1:8). The New Testament records that they weren't the only ones to receive empowerment from the Holy Spirit more than once.

Could I? I had undoubtedly received the Holy Spirit at the time of my baptism. Was there *more* of the Holy Spirit that I could—and needed to—ask for?

Was the Luke 11 teaching of Jesus on prayer showing me the way for me to cooperate with God so that the energy of Christ could work powerfully through *me* (Colossians 1:29)? Have I lacked God's power because I did not know I needed to *ask him for it?*

Well, now I know. And the need feels visceral, urgent. So I pray a prayer like that of 2 Thessalonians 1:11–12 over my own life:

> So we keep on praying for you, asking our God to enable you to live a life worthy of his call. May he give you the power to accomplish all the good things your faith prompts you to do. Then the name of our Lord Jesus will be honored because of the way you live....
>
> 2 THESSALONIANS 1:11–12

11

Loving Christ

A snippet of a Christian song came sailing through the air to my ears one afternoon. The lyrics were meant to encourage believers with the truth that this life is but a vapor and we'll soon be home-free. As the chorus reached me, however, my initial reaction was mixed.

I was, of course, excited at how great Heaven is going to be, and the reminder of that was quite positive. But that reaction was superseded by an urgent desire for something *else* first.

I *want* a spiritually fruitful life. I *want* to participate in the kingdom of God the way I was designed to, and put here for.

God had used one line of a song to check the temperature of my heart for Christ.

Except for the dentist's drill in my mouth, it was a really good moment.

Not Yet

That night, I went to bed with tears on my pillow.

God had set me to the frequency of compassion for a certain population of unhealed people. And I had become convinced, by the Scriptures and by the credible testimonies of others alive in my generation, that God wants to, and can, heal many of them in this life—through believers in Christ.

> *And then he told them, "Go into all the world and preach the Good News to everyone. Anyone who believes and is baptized will be saved. ... These miraculous signs will accompany those who believe: ... They will be able to place their hands on the sick, and they will be healed."*
> MARK 16:15–18

But there is still a gap between my compassion and my spiritual preparation to be a conduit for God's power. It is becoming more and more unacceptable to me for that gap to remain. Yet, it is a chasm that can only be spanned by his power, his guidance—*his Spirit*. And so, I prayed, with tears, "You can't leave me here."

This wasn't a prayer for my own healing. Not even a little. It was a cry for God to fulfill his call on my life. It was my spirit's cry that *I can't continue to live unequipped*—*I want to live the life you made me for*.

I hadn't arrived anywhere. But it felt like I was finally getting near the *starting* point of something.

Bringing the Kingdom Near

The next night, I was thinking of Isaiah's prophecies about Christ—about how Messiah would set the oppressed free, remove the chains that bound people, and remove the heavy yoke of oppression (Isaiah 58:6, 9). Christ had stood up and read those very prophecies aloud in the synagogue in Nazareth. He had proclaimed that *he* was the one of whom Isaiah had spoken, and that the time had arrived for those things to commence (Luke 4:16–21).

And then Jesus had gone around *healing* thousands and thousands of people.

Isaiah's prophecies hadn't been just symbolic, or merely poetic: Jesus lived them out. Unhealed physical conditions *are* a form of spiritual and physical oppression. By healing people, Jesus *was* making the captives and the oppressed free. He was *destroying the works of the devil* (1 John 3:8).

Jesus even taught his first disciples to tell the people they healed that *the kingdom of God had come near to them* (Matthew 10:7; Luke 10:9).

God *wants* his kingdom to come on earth. It's why Jesus taught the calling forth of God's kingdom—*your kingdom come*—as one of the first parts of prayer (Matthew 6:10 NKJV).

Jesus is not finished with that work. So neither are we (John 14:12).

This is How I Love Christ

If Jesus were standing here in a physical body in front of his sick brothers and sisters today, I am fully confident that millions of *unhealed* people would be *healed*. He would put his hands on their ears, or apply clay to their eyes, or let them touch the hem of his robe, or take them by the hand, or give them a command to stand up and walk—or some other thing—*and they would be healed*. The work of the devil would be destroyed.

It slowly dawned on me then that *this is how I love Christ: I love him by cooperating with him in what he wants to do to bring his healing to captives of illness and these oppressed by disease.*

Whatever you do for my sick brothers and sisters, you do for me, Christ said (Matthew 25:36, author's paraphrase). Working with Jesus to *set them free and break their yoke of oppression*—because of compassion for them—is what he was asking me to do (see Isaiah 58:6; 1 John 3:18). And *doing it* will be *loving him*.

This is so important to God, so central to his will, that Paul went so far as to characterize the demonstration of power that *is* miraculous signs and wonders—largely including healing—as part of the work of *fully presenting the gospel* (1 Thessalonians 1:5; Romans 15:19; Acts 19:11–12)—work that Christ's followers are now tasked to do (see 2 Corinthians 5:20).

Healing is a vital part of the *show* portion of the *show and tell* message that *is* living by God's power. "For the Kingdom of God is not just a lot of talk; it is living by God's power" (1 Corinthians 4:20).

And there is not even one component of that that I can, in my power, do. Every part of it, humanly, is impossible.

In my own power, I can't heal people of their complex, longstanding unhealed physical conditions. In my own power, I can't even love them—especially not the way Jesus did. God will be the *source* of all of it.

But even though God will be the *source* of the power, I *will* have work to do. Didn't Paul say he *worked* and *struggled so hard*, even *while* he was "depending on Christ's mighty power" working within him (Colossians 1:29)?

What *would* my task be? What kind of work had God prepared long ago for me to do?[1]

12

My Isaac

I've heard that when your heart goes out to someone, Jesus is asking you to do something.

I know his heart has already gone out. When I consider the sick people I know, and the millions more I don't know, it makes me think of Jesus's response in Matthew 9:36: "When he saw the crowds, he had compassion on them because they were confused and helpless, like sheep without a shepherd."

The unhealed today are weary, as well—from sickness and from every problem that comes *with* it and *from* it. It's a spiritual assault, as well as physical oppression.

For those who are *not yet* children of God, and also for those who are, God's compassion poured into them through his healing power could open their spirits to receive his love in a way that would make an eternal difference—not just a temporal difference—to them (see Mark 16:20; John 4:48; 10:37–38; Acts 14:3; Romans 15:18–19; Hebrews 2:3–4).

Gifts of Healing

While *every* Christian is capable of praying in faith for the healing of others (James 5:16), the Spirit also gives *gifts of healing* to certain individuals to help others (1 Corinthians 12:7, 9).[1]

Although the Spirit of God *decides* who will receive such a gift of healing (1 Corinthians 12:11), Paul taught that believers should *eagerly desire the gifts of the Spirit* (1 Corinthians 14:1) that will strengthen the whole church (1 Corinthians 14:12).

From this vantage point, looking in every direction, it appears that that spiritual gifts of healing and miracles are *especially* needed to strengthen the church in this generation.

Some in this generation already *have* spiritual gifts of healing and are stewarding them well. But I am convinced that God intended for there to be *many more* believers using healing gifts.

Look at the order in which Paul says God has ranked the gifts of miracles and healing in in the church: "And God has placed in the church first of all apostles, second prophets, third teachers, then miracles, then gifts of healing…" (1 Corinthians 12:28). Fourth and fifth. Since spiritual gifts *build up the church* (1 Corinthians 14:12), this ranking of gifts of healing indicates just *how* vital *healing* is to building up the church.

Miracles and healing are both among the *greater gifts* that Paul teaches believers to eagerly desire (1 Corinthians 12:31; 14:1). And there wouldn't be any point in *eagerly desiring* certain gifts if the desire couldn't be fulfilled. Therefore, when we see a need for gifts to build up the church, we should *ask God*.

God, please raise up many with the gifts of healing and miracles. We have a great need for healing of sick people inside and outside the church. Many of the workers are sick, and the harvest fields are full of sick people, too! Send out more workers with the gifts of miracles and healing! (See Matthew 9:35–38.)

Where I Fit

Although the overall need seemed glaringly obvious, it was less clear to me exactly where God might want *me* to fit into that picture, and what I should ask from him regarding my own life.

I wrestled with the question: Was *I* willing to receive and steward *any spiritual gift he might want to give me*, in order to help some of these unhealed people?[2]

I already *had* a concept of how I thought God might use me in his kingdom, and of the kind of spiritual gifting that I thought would fit with that. In fact, I had believed that call was from God, and I had been actively pursuing it.

But what if God wanted to do something else?

I could think of many reasons that I really *wouldn't* be a good fit for certain kinds of kingdom work, and a much *better* fit for other kinds. But so could Moses think of many reasons he wouldn't be a good candidate *for the very task he had been born for* (see Exodus 4:10–17).

I had to leave room for the possibility that God had his eye on something for my future that I hadn't even thought of yet. Even when I may see in part, I still do not have the full picture (1 Corinthians 13:9).

Therefore, I didn't *know* how to pray. *Should I continue to just pursue the dreams and callings I thought he had given me, and the gifting that seemed to go with that? Should I set aside that vision to ask for something else? If so, what?* Maybe God really did want some option for my life that I hadn't even thought of.

I asked God, but he seemed silent.

How could I even decide what to pray?

I was wearing myself out trying to figure out what to pray for my own life. I knew that no vision would come to be unless God equipped and empowered me by his Spirit. Yet, God *has* given humans the responsibility, privilege, and power of participating with him through prayer.

I finally realized—*thank you, Holy Spirit* (Romans 8:26; 1 Corinthians 2:10–11)—that what I *needed* to pray in this particular situation was for God to gift and empower me by his Spirit and use me to build up the church in whatever way fit with his design.

PS My Healing

I was a little surprised to notice that, as I wrestled with these spiritual matters, my own physical healing was *not* foremost in my thoughts. It entered in only as being a logistic God would need to handle if it got in the way of his design.

I certainly hadn't *forgotten* that I was in need of healing; I now had renewed faith to pray and to seek prayer for my own complete healing, and I regularly did so. But my own physical healing was a *different* issue than this matter of spiritual gifting and empowerment for God's call, and it was this matter that had taken precedence in my heart. At the center of my attention was how God wanted to work with me and wanted me to work with him to build his kingdom.

But as I continued to pray prayers—like that in 2 Thessalonians 1:11 and this one from Hebrews 13—for my own life, I came to recognize that the "may he equip you with all you need for doing his will" of this prayer encompassed *everything* I needed to do God's will:

> Now may the God of peace—who brought up from the dead our Lord Jesus, the great Shepherd of the sheep, and ratified an eternal covenant with his blood—may he equip you with all you need for doing his will. May he produce in you, through the power of Jesus Christ, every good thing that is pleasing to him. All glory to him forever and ever! Amen.
> HEBREWS 13:20–21

If my healing was among the "all" that would be needed to carry out God's will for my life, then it was included.

My Isaac on the Altar

To honestly pray for God to use me however he wanted, I would need to *Abraham my Isaac* (see Genesis 22)—willingly placing my future—and my dreams—on an altar to God (Romans 12:1). God would be the one to say what would happen next.

I would ask God for his will (instead of mine) where there was any divergence, and to redirect me if he wanted to. I *wanted* him to adjust me so that *my* will and spirit would align with *his* will and Spirit.

He knows the full parameters of *his* design for my life and how that fits with the life of his kingdom (see Ephesians 2:10; Jeremiah 1:5). I had come far enough to know that I didn't *want* to pursue any vision other than one he had chosen for me—whatever that was.

And so I would take my Isaac up the mountain. If God *wanted* a different type of future for me than the one I had envisioned—even though I thought he had called me to it—then I would not come back down Moriah with that vision. He would give me another one, and empower me to live it out. But if God said, *Pick up that vision; take it and live it*, then by his power, he would enable me to do it. Either way, we'd both know that I had not withheld this from him (Genesis 22:10–12).

I realized, with a sort of small shock, that this trip up the mountain to lay my future before God was only a *little* about obedience, and *not only* about trust. This was faith, expressing itself in *love*.

I wanted to hear about *his dreams*. I wanted *his heart*. I wanted *him*.

And he had prepared the way.

God had seen my desire to turn around the wedges in our relationship and to make them work *for* us. He had responded by consistently blowing away lies and tearing down walls that had come between us.

He had opened my heart to him in so many ways that this trip up the mountain wasn't a slow trudge at all. I was eager to meet him, to hear from him.

My heart flew there in anticipation.

Note from the Author

Visit https://amylu-riley.com to read articles, join my email community, and find recommendations for further reading.

For the stories before this one, read *Stay: Why I'm Still Here, A Spiritual Memoir* and *Faith with Grit for the Not-Yet Healed*.

Acknowledgements

I have so much gratitude for the people who have been *for me* during the living and the writing of this book.

Richard Riley, I love you so much. You are a treasure and I am eternally grateful to God for you. Thank you so much for your continual love and support for me and my writing. Thank you also for your specific technical and creative contributions to the cover of this book; you turned my vision into art.

To my beloved family, Bea and Merle Rice, Jon and Angie Rice, Josh Rice, Zach Rice, and Charlene and Ken Roth, thank you for your encouragement, love, prayers, and support. I am so grateful for you and to you. I love you all.

Jennifer Bagby, I thank God for you and for the way you see with spiritual eyes and speak words of faith.

Danée Morel, I am grateful for you and for how God has brought us from where we began our lives with him together, to being together again where we are now.

Greg Allen and Mary Allen, my deepest gratitude to you both for being a vital part of this journey. And many thanks to Greg for reading and giving feedback on a manuscript of this book.

I am deeply grateful for the significant contributions that the ministries and writing of Susie Larson, Francis MacNutt, and

Craig S. Keener have made to my life. I thank God for each of them and for their work.

To Deana Rehmel, Marcia Mills, Dalynn Haney, Dorolyn Haney, and every friend who has encouraged me and helped me by your prayers, thank you.

And to Connie Stambush and to the Create Ifs, my writing community, thank you for your camaraderie.

Chapter 1 – For the Love of God

1. If Jesus were writing a letter to me like those in Revelation 2 and 3, what could he say about my love for him?
2. How are my complaints against God connected to my answer to question 1?
3. What do I need to ask God for help with?

Chapter 2 – Can God Be Trusted?

1. How is suffering getting in the way of my trusting God?
2. In what areas has my trust in God drifted?
3. In order for me to trust God, what do I need to ask him to show me?

Chapter 3 – Demolition

1. What circumstantial evidence seems to be piling up that I am on my own and God won't be intervening for me?
2. In what area have I stopped asking God for help?
3. Am I ready to ask God now to reveal lies to me and replace them with the truth?

Chapter 4 – Commissioned

1. Why is it important that the work of Christ is to destroy the work of the devil?
2. Who gets free when the work of the devil is destroyed? (Consider Isaiah 58:6.)
3. Am I ready to ask God to work in me and through me?

Chapter 5 – Awakening

1. What miracles have I experienced or witnessed?
2. Do I have questions about how to carry out my role as a believer in Jesus, as Jesus described in John 14:12–14?
3. Am I ready to ask God to address my questions and any doubts?

Chapter 6 – What Does God Want?

1. How does God in my real life seem different from God in the Bible?
2. Do the Scriptures presented throughout this chapter convince me that God generally wants to heal?
3. Am I ready to effectively pray the prayer of faith for another believer as described in James 5:16–18?

Chapter 7 – Case Not Closed

1. How is the prayer of faith described in this chapter different from the way I pray for healing?

2. How did I react to learn from Scripture that someone might remain unhealed because Jesus's disciples couldn't heal him or her—even though God *wanted* to heal?
3. Am I ready to ask God to show me how I can live in such a way as to be a more effective conduit of God's power?

Chapter 8 – Seeing the Battlefield

1. What are some practical ways I can increase my faith?
2. How would I describe the substance of my prayers? What am I putting into those bowls in heaven?
3. Am I ready to ask God to show me anything I still need to forgive?

Chapter 9 – Active Duty

1. How does it change my thinking about my own life to realize that Paul *started the Galatian church* while his health was broken?
2. How does the story of the opposition to Nehemiah's work (see Nehemiah 1–7) change my view of my own circumstances?
3. Am I ready to ask God to show me how to fully live into the design he has for me?

Chapter 10 – Power

1. Can I relate to Paul's description in Colossians 1:29 of the power working within him?

2. Given the relationship between the power of God and the Holy Spirit (see Acts 6:8), is it possible that I may need to ask God for an increase of the Holy Spirit in me?
3. Am I ready to pray 2 Thessalonians 1:11–12 for my own life?

Chapter 11 – Loving Christ

1. How spiritually fruitful is my life?
2. If Jesus were standing here in an earthly body in front of my sick brother or sister, what do I think he would do and say?
3. Do I sense God calling me to help bring his kingdom to earth in some way that I haven't before?

Chapter 12 – My Isaac

1. To whom is my heart going out?
2. Am I ready to pray—for the local church and the global church—the prayer at the end of the "Gifts of Healing" section of this chapter?
3. Am I ready to pray—for my own life—the prayer at the end of the "PS My Healing" section of this chapter?

Notes

Chapter 1
For the Love of God

1. Some believe that Paul's thorn was a physical health problem, such as malaria (John Wilkinson, *The Bible and Healing: A Medical and Theological Commentary*, (Eerdmans Pub Co., 2000)) or some other infirmity. Others have postulated that the thorn was *not* sickness, but human opposition to Paul's work (John Wimber and Kevin Springer, *Power Healing* (HarperOne, 1987)). My present position is to regard the thorn as a physical affliction, in part because of the following:

- God and Paul both use the word *weakness* (Greek: *astheneiais*) in direct reference to Paul's thorn in the flesh (2 Corinthians 12:9).
- In 2 Corinthians 12:10, Paul lists his *weaknesses* as separate items from *the insults, hardships, persecutions, and troubles* in a list of things he suffers for Christ.

My book *Faith with Grit for the Not-Yet Healed* (AmyLu Riley, 2019) contains an in-depth discussion regarding Paul's thorn.

Chapter 2
Can God Be Trusted?

1. Hebrews 11:32–39 teaches that sometimes faith leads to apparent victory (Hebrews 11:33–35) and sometimes the faithful live with what looks like a loss (Hebrews 11:35–38). *All* of those mentioned in Hebrews 11 were commended for their faith. But faith doesn't guarantee a comfortable *short-term* outcome. *Everything* God has promised to the faithful is not received in *this* life (Hebrews 11:39).

2. See John chapters 11–14 and 17 for the domino effect of events begun by the raising of Lazarus from the dead. Scripture says that the outcome of all those events was the reason Lazarus's death was permitted by God at that time. I explore this sequence of events in detail in *Faith with Grit for the Not-Yet Healed* (AmyLu Riley, 2019), on pages 42, 197–198.

3. I am grateful to John Eldredge and Brent Curtis for their discussion of *rescue* in the book *The Sacred Romance: Drawing Closer to the Heart of God* (Nashville: Thomas Nelson, 1997), which God used to open my understanding to other, related concepts.

4. Job received reassurance from God that Job's suffering was not caused by any of the things his friends had previously suggested (Job 42:7); that what Job had said about God had all

been correct (Job 42:7–8); and that Job was in right standing with God (Job 42:8–9).

5. The moment will come when everything will be set right (Revelation 21:4). 1 Corinthians 15:52–54 says, "It will happen in a moment, in the blink of an eye, when the last trumpet is blown. For when the trumpet sounds, those who have died will be raised to live forever. And we who are living will also be transformed. For our dying bodies must be transformed into bodies that will never die; our mortal bodies must be transformed into immortal bodies. Then, when our dying bodies have been transformed into bodies that will never die, this Scripture will be fulfilled: 'Death is swallowed up in victory.'"

Chapter 3
Demolition

1. I am grateful to Susie Larson for her excellent book *Fully Alive* (Bloomington, Minnesota: Bethany House Publishers, 2018).

2. See Job 33:14–18.

Chapter 5
Awakening

1. Craig S. Keener, *Miracles: The Credibility of the New Testament Accounts* (Ada, Michigan: Baker Publishing Group, 2011).

2. Francis MacNutt, *The Healing Reawakening: Reclaiming Our Lost Inheritance* (Ada, Michigan: Chosen Books, 2006).

3. Chronic disease statistic: Centers for Disease Control and Prevention, accessed February 13, 2020, https://www.cdc.gov/chronicdisease/resources/infographic/chronic-diseases.htm. (According to the page, content was last reviewed on October 23, 2019.)

United States population in 2019 (the year when the CDC's statistic immediately above was last updated) was 329,064,917. Source: Worldometer, accessed February 13, 2020, https://www.worldometers.info/world-population/us-population/.

4. Cother Hajat and Emma Stein, "The Global Burden of Multiple Chronic Conditions: A Narrative Review." *Prev Med Rep.*, 12 (Dec 2018) 284-293, https://www.ncbi.nlm.nih.gov/pmc/articles/PMC6214883/.

5. Source: Agnes Sanford CFO lectures, accessed February 14, 2020, https://www.cfoclassicslibrary.org. Also see Bill Johnson, *Face to Face with God* (Lake Mary, Florida: Charisma House, 2015).

Chapter 6
What Does God Want?

1. Not even in the case of Paul's thorn did God indicate that it was *not his will* to heal. I discuss this in depth in my book *Faith with Grit for the Not-Yet Healed* (AmyLu Riley, 2019).

2. See Keener, *Miracles*, 2011.

3. A careful reading of James 5:14–16 will reveal that it speaks clearly for itself about the conditions of its own fulfillment—many of which are incumbent upon *those praying* for the sick person.

4. I say *generally* to leave room for three things: 1) The end of a life, at the God-appointed time, of one God loves, such as, for example, King David (1 Kings 1:1; 2:10). 2) The end of a life of one who has irrevocably chosen to be God's enemy, such as King Saul. God did not heal Saul from his battle wound, for God had been the one to kill Saul (1 Chronicles 10:3–4, 14). 3) Spiritual principles beyond my current understanding.

5. Even when Jesus waited until after sick Lazarus *died* to come to him, Jesus's *intention* from the beginning was to heal him, and he *did* heal him (John 11). In *Faith with Grit* (AmyLu Riley, 2019), I discuss in more depth the reasons that God delayed Lazarus's healing, and what God brought out of the delay.

6. The man mentioned in Acts 3:2–8 had surely been around when incarnate Jesus was healing people; yet he was not healed until Peter and John went to him later, acting with Jesus's authority, and healed him. To those who say Jesus did not heal everyone alive while he walked the earth, I think this account reinforces the reality that Jesus intended his healing work to be continued by his followers, exactly as he had trained them to do and as this healing was done.

7. God *will* give sufficient grace to his people to live unhealed, as he did to Paul. In addition, God will bring good from even evil: "All things work together for good to those who love God, to those who are the called according to His purpose" (Romans 8:28 NKJV). It is also true that Christians can be matured by perseverance in suffering in a way that produces character and hope (Romans 5:3–5). But see chapter 5 regarding suffering in the form of persecution versus suffering in the form of sickness. None of that, however,

means that God still doesn't will to heal, or that if a healing hasn't happened yet, that it must never happen.

8. God has permitted the free will of his creation to be exercised to such a degree that God's will is not always done—evil is done, and much good is left undone. Free will of humankind also means that God will not force himself on people who do not want him; see Matthew 13:58; Mark 6:5; Luke 9:52–56. However, God's *purposes* will always ultimately prevail (Proverbs 19:21; 21:30; Romans 8:28).

9. Francis MacNutt wrote encouragingly and informatively on the topic of increasing our individual effectiveness in healing ministry, in *The Power to Heal* (Notre Dame, Indiana: Ave Maria Press, 1977). I recommend the book for its practical and compassionate help in this and other key areas.

10. Francis MacNutt's *Healing* (Notre Dame, Indiana: Ave Maria Press, 1974) outlines a number of reasons he discovered that healing does not take place; and a later work of his, *The Power to Heal* (1977), added further important insights to that list.

Someone may also ask about God's will to heal in cases when it is a person's appointed time to die (see Ecclesiastes 3:2 and Hebrews 9:27). In the writings of Agnes Sanford (*The Healing Light*, 1947) and Francis MacNutt (*The Power to Heal*), they both wisely point out the need for discernment on the part of the person praying. They recommend consulting with God before asking for any specific person's healing, to discern when a person should *not* pray for a particular person's physical healing.

(Both writers gave examples of kinds of prayers that may be appropriate in end-of-life instances, because they are encouraging, comforting, and helpful to the spirit of the person being prayed for.)

Sanford also discussed frankly in her writings that there are also other particular spiritual scenarios—besides end-of-life—that are reasons God may direct a certain person not to pray for another specific individual's healing at a certain time. Those topics are outside the scope of this book, but they were important enough that, in Sanford's experience, asking God first whether she were the one to pray for a person's healing, and whether this was the time to pray for it—and then following his guidance—was the wise and recommended course of action.

One last point about end-of-life: I think it is also significant to note that while Scripture is clear that humans *will* die (Hebrews 9:27), and while, in our generation, unhealed sickness has played a central role in bringing about death, it is equally clear from Scripture that humans don't *require* sickness in order to fulfill our appointments with death. Humans *can* die without being sick (see Deuteronomy 34:7).

11. The full presentation of the Good News is not only for those who have not yet heard about Jesus. Paul taught that the spiritual gifts God provided to the church were given to strengthen the church (Romans 1:11; 1 Corinthians 14:12).

12. See John 5:19.

Chapter 7
Case Not Closed

1. In *The Power to Heal* (1977), Francis MacNutt recounted a number of cases from his own Christian healing ministry in which people with longstanding health issues were healed through repeated prayers over a period of time, a practice MacNutt termed *soaking prayer*. He explained how prayer for hours in a single day, or repeated daily or weekly (for minutes or longer periods at one time) had been used in slow, gradual—and observable—healings of chronic health issues, including physical conditions in which improvement is typically not seen. MacNutt made the point that praying in this way is work, and can take months or years.

He addressed the reality that many people think healing must occur instantaneously if it is going to occur, and are not aware that slow, gradual healing through persistent, ongoing prayer is a way that God works. MacNutt cited Scripture in which Jesus urges believers to be persistent in prayer.

(See *The Power to Heal* for descriptions of techniques MacNutt used for the type of soaking prayer that he saw effectively carried out during his years of Christian healing ministry, as well as several extremely encouraging testimonies.)

There are too many people living with chronic illness for us to remain ignorant that God has done healing this way and could reasonably be expected to do so again.

2. Agnes Sanford, *Behold Your God* (Austin, Minnesota: Macalester Park Publishing Co., 1958).

3. God expected Jesus's healing ministry to *continue* through those who believe in Christ. See also Chapter 6, note #6, above.

In addition, some of those God *would* have healed were *not* healed, because they refused to cooperate with God; (see Matthew 13:58, Mark 6:5, Luke 9:52–53).

4. I make this assumption based on Saul's original reason for going to Damascus: to arrest both male and female followers

of Christ and bring them back to Jerusalem to be killed (Acts 9:1–2).

5. Sarah J. Thiessen discusses quantum physics and prayer in *Splankna: The Redemption of Energy Healing for the Kingdom of God* (Bloomington, Indiana: WestBow Press, 2017) and in her earlier book, with Heather Hughes, *UpperDogs: Christians Have the Advantage. It's Time to Take It.* (Bloomington, Indiana: WestBow Press, 2015).

William L. DeArteaga discusses quantum physics and faith in chapter 10 ("Quantum Physics and Spirituality") of his book *Agnes Sanford and Her Companions* (Eugene, Oregon: Wipf & Stock, 2015).

Chapter 8
Seeing the Battlefield

1. One is not shielded from all physical trouble (John 16:33) or persecution (John 15:20), so I interpret 1 Peter 1:5 as spiritual protection, viewing it through the lens of 2 Timothy 4:18, in which Paul (who had not been shielded from a life of physical trouble and persecution) states that the Lord will *deliver him from every evil attack*.

2. See Ephesians 6:10–18 for teaching on faith as a shield, as well as other spiritual armor: truth, righteousness, the peace that comes from the Good News, salvation, the Word of God, and prayer in the Spirit.

Tested faith that has become purified and strengthened will also be made to serve a new purpose when the fight is over: It will bring reward (1 Peter 1:6–7).

3. For some recommended resources on these topics, see https://amylu-riley.com.

Chapter 9
Active Duty

1. In his *Revelation Audio Lectures* (Grand Rapids, Michigan: Zondervan Academic, 2017), Craig S. Keener makes the point that while John wasn't permitted to leave Patmos, he could have visitors.

2. Around us are people for whom God is waiting (Hebrews 11:39–40). God loves them enough that all of the suffering of humankind weighs less on his scales than would the loss of their souls. (See Colossians 3:1–2.)

Chapter 10
Power

1. Craig S. Keener has written beautifully and accessibly on this topic in his book *Gift and Giver: The Holy Spirit for Today* (Ada, Michigan: Baker Books, 2001). He also helps clear a path

for understanding by addressing confusion about the terminology used to discuss the topic.

Chapter 11
Loving Christ

1. See Ephesians 2:10.

Chapter 12
My Isaac

1. Another mechanism for healing was also given by God to the church, and that is the prayer in faith of the church elders, with anointing of oil, as described in James 5:14–15. I discuss that in *Faith with Grit for the Not-Yet Healed* (AmyLu Riley, 2019).

2. I am grateful to Craig S. Keener for his framing of the concept (in *Gift & Giver*, 2001) of asking God to give people those spiritual gifts that one sees are needed in the church—and to be willing to be one of those people.

Also by AmyLu Riley

Faith with Grit

"I know God can heal me, so why doesn't he?" That one spiritual issue can cause more hurt than many physical problems combined. Maybe you're facing this. While your faith is a lifeline, something painful just isn't adding up. Come on a quest for the kind of faith *your* spirit needs to live strong.

Stay: Why I'm Still Here, A Spiritual Memoir

AmyLu wanted God to show her what she needed to accomplish in this life so she could just do it and be free to go home. But God didn't want a transaction. He wanted a restoration. You're invited into an intimate inner journey. Be encouraged by seeing how God took what looked like an ending and quietly made it into a new beginning. Just like he wants to do for you.

Visit https://amylu-riley.com for information.

Made in the USA
Columbia, SC
23 June 2020